JOY café

REDISCOVERING COMMUNITY, CONNECTION AND BELONGING

Dr. Jeff Williamson

Paperback ISBN: 979-8-218-42461-9

Digital ISNB: 979-8-218-43095-5

Cover Art by Kevin Williamson Design

Published by CMG Group Inc.

Chicago, IL

Table of Contents

Praise for Joy Café

I feel as if I'm sitting across from you at a coffee shop with a good cup of coffee, and we're having a conversation. If that was one of your goals in your writing, I think you hit it out of the ballpark. The balance of storytelling and insight was excellent.

Jim E. Johnson, Vice-President of Business Development, CVC Communications Inc.

As someone who's just written her own book, I can tell you that I felt every word you wrote about your grief (particularly the grief of your dad).

I think connection and belonging are definitely something that resonated with me... Your book has inspired me... I know that I was created for connection and all of the stories within your book just reiterated that to me!

Leslie Weirich, Author of "The Gifts of Grief", Keynote Speaker, Suicide Prevention Advocate

Joy Cafe bridges the gap between the lonely COVID 2020 era and today by reminding us of our need for community and connection. Jeff takes us on a compelling and engaging "comeback tour" with stories of his personal sorrow and growth and points us towards practical ways to experience our own "comeback".

We get to join him as he uses coffee and locally owned cafes to demonstrate how loneliness and grief can be used for good by pointing us to one another. I recommend you get the book, head to your local cafe, order the hand-crafted latte, and cherish the quiet as you travel on this quest for joy.

Amy Zabel, Career Coach, HR Professional, Founder, Podcast Host

The story was so well written, so vivid. I could see the restaurant and the family sitting at the kitchen table. It really hit home for me in my last few years of life and having lost a parent and multiple close friends.

Jeff Williams, Chairman & CEO, Spry Inc.

This book is a calm exhale. For one, it's in the way you saw each of these amazing families. We see them through your eyes ... what it all meant to you... which IS feeling you and your presence. We're feeling your healing. And within that... it's allowing our own exhale. It's like being brought through a beautiful vision softly through time...It's classic... it's timeless... I could read it over again. This is a walk in a familiar park. It IS the afternoon at the favorite coffee shop. You have done it.

Emily Sifrit, Fashion Designer, E.Kaye
Senior Consultant, Pleneri Inc.

Our life stories are unique. Where we are born . . . how we live our life . . . even how we die. Through times of gathering with friends and strangers after isolation, Jeff shares in "Joy Café" the heartfelt life lessons he learned on his personal journey to feel connections with others. From café owners to Jeff's own memories, you'll easily find the importance of deep-rooted relationships for your own life.

Meegan Siegwarth, Vice-President of Marketing & Member Experience,
Interra Credit Union

When I first heard about Jeff's plan to share coffee time with various people at various locations around the country, my first reaction was, "You must write a book about your experiences!" I'm so glad he has recorded so many special connections in the pages of his new book. Readers will be blessed, challenged, and encouraged by the stories he shares. From one connector to another, thanks for connecting all of us through your book, Jeff.

Laura Wasson Warfel
Writer for 989 Group
Founder and Chief Encouragement Officer for More Than A Widow

Dr. Jeff Williamson takes a deep look at his life through a coffee filtered lens. Jeff rediscovers himself while traveling through 15 states and 60 different cafés.

While on his journey Jeff shares his personal thoughts on joy, grief, culture, faith, values, sadness, and death. His final cup, Jeff highlights the importance of community, connection and belonging... life's recipe for Joy.

A heartfelt book that is a must read for anyone looking for life's deeper meaning!

Jeff Christian, Author, "We Rise Together" and "Lucy's Secret Sauce"
Founder & CEO, C4 Leaders

Dr. Jeff brilliantly tells his story of loss and the soul-wrenching pain that comes from grief. Though he is able to take you on his journey of sadness, he generously shares his moments of love for his family and communities which are so vividly depicted in a way that makes you feel like you are traveling the Midwest and beyond with him. His message of hope for restoration to joy and connection will resonate with us all.

Chasity Wells-Armstrong, Catalyst Coaching & Transformation,
Former Mayor of Kankakee, IL

This book offers a warm invitation to its reader to embark on a journey not only on a quest for a great cup of coffee, but also in search of something every human needs: connection. Jeff shares personal anecdotes and growth markers to bring the reader along on this beautiful adventure. I'm sure you'll find as I did that this read is time well spent!

-Sarah Fenlon Falk, Author

About the Author

He holds a bachelor's, and master's degree in Speech Communication, and a Doctor of Education degree (Ed.D.) in Educational Leadership and was a post-doctoral student at The Ohio State University, *Fisher College of Business*. He is the host of "Leadership LevelUp" podcast and is also a Gallup-certified Strengths Coach.

He regularly teaches and speaks to business and industry on topics such as: Personal Leadership, Leadership Paradigms, Leading Change, Discover Your Strengths, Building a Strengths-Based Organization, Coaching, Mentoring & Conflict Resolution.

Connect with Jeff on social media:

LinkedIn: *https://www.linkedin.com/in/jeffreyswilliamson/*

Facebook: *https://www.facebook.com/jeff.williamson.372661*

Instagram: *https://www.instagram.com/drjeffwilliamson/*

Converge Group website: *www.convergegroup.io*

To book Jeff for your next event, please go to:

www.convergegroup.io/get-started/

Dedication

This book is dedicated in loving memory of my parents, Kenneth & Betty Williamson. I loved being your son, our life on Schooner Valley, and the never-ending support and unconditional love that have shaped who I am. You live in the pages of these stories and will always live in my heart and be with me through every day to come.

Acknowledgements

With any project like this, there are plenty of "thank you's" and gratitude to go around. Many different people have played a part in the beginnings, the "land between" when I could not generate much of anything, and those who cheered me on in the home stretch with the writing and telling of this story.

In the pages that follow, besides my parents, Ken and Betty, you will meet my siblings, and some of my extended family who were so significant in my growing up years. Each of the Williamson and Powell clans are a part of my story and who I am.

I also want to express my appreciation to my friends, Staci Wilken and Sarah Marion who were a part of the early days of The Coffee Tour. Your continued friendship and encouragement have been so appreciated.

As my manuscript was beginning to take shape, I had multiple conversations with Amelia Forczak, who is a gifted writer, editor and writing coach whose early insights and her suggestion that I "write myself into the story" was a game-changer. That was a pivot point that helped this book come alive and become what it is now.

To my advance reader team who gave of yourselves and your time, I'm so grateful. The insights, edits, suggestions, and affirmations were so helpful, and meaningful. Thank you for your patience with my frequent texts, emails, and reminders when we were approaching deadlines. I'm honored by your friendship and your gift of time. Those readers were: Sarah Falk, Jim E. Johnson, Rob Kee, Laura Warfel, Leslie Weirich, Meegan Siegwarth, Jeff Williams, Amy Zabel, Emily Sifrit, Jeff Christian, and Chasity Wells-Armstrong.

Finally, my gratitude and appreciation to my wife Mindy, and our children Jordan, Jayna, and Kate who have been our "why" since the beginning. The four of you have walked through many parts of this story, and for better or worse, have had a front-row seat to witness my struggles, losses, and failures as well as my victories, and achievements. Thank you for standing with me and loving me in spite of myself. I am forever grateful.

Introduction

There is an old photograph, from December 1965, and I am standing on a small wooden stool in front of a classic white and blue Chambers gas stove, with a wooden-handled spatula in hand on my 4th birthday. It wasn't a staged shot I'm told; I simply wanted to make the cheeseburgers for my own birthday party. I don't recall that conversation with my mom, yet there I was in the picture; checkered shirt and jeans, burger buns prepared to my right, cooking cheeseburgers for my family in one of those classic black cast iron skillets.

As long as I can remember, I have equated connection with simple time spent together, perhaps sharing food, or a hot cup of coffee around a table, where there was a sense of joy, love, appreciation, and belonging. It was a place where there was laughter, storytelling, some occasional, good-natured "ribbing" of each other, and having *a place* where I knew I was *somebody* to the others around the table.

There are two pictures from that day. One is up close of me at the stove, and then a similar picture from a wider perspective that shows some of those present. In the background of the second picture, sitting at the table are my Great Uncle Herman Powell, Great Aunt Annie Powell, and a precious lady we all called Grandma Durham (Annie's mother). I loved Herman, Annie, and Grandma Durham, and they loved me. The three of them played a major role in my life growing up. Grandma Durham seemed to have thought I could do no wrong. I would often stay at their house on the farm a few miles away near a tiny crossroads with a gas station, and bait shop known as Belmont. She and I would play games in the front living room, and somehow, I *always* beat her at checkers, and she would smile and giggle and say "Oh, you've beaten me again". At a young age I didn't realize she was letting me win, *every single time.*

Besides my 4th birthday party dinner, we shared many meals with the Powell and Williamson clan. Less than a year later, we had been at Herman and Annie's house for dinner one night with them and Grandma Durham. Just a couple of hours later, our phone rang, with the news that Grandma Durham collapsed, fell out of her chair at the kitchen table, and passed away from an apparent heart attack.

As a little 5-year-old boy who adored her, I struggled to grasp how she could be gone, when my dad told me she had passed away. In my child's mind, I recall thinking "How can she be gone? I just saw her at dinner." That is my earliest memory of losing someone I loved, and I have sweet memories of her, even all these years later.

My Aunt Annie, had me ride with her and Uncle Herman in the limousine as we drove from Grandma Durham's funeral service to the burial. Though I don't remember that part, Annie often told me that having me with her on the worst day of her life was a comfort and a healthy distraction from her grief and sadness.

I didn't really know then what grief was, or the sadness that comes from losing a parent or someone who we love, but those indelible memories remain even five plus decades later. Grandma Durham found such joy in that little boy, and early on I learned from my parents, siblings and many extended family members, just what it felt like to be deeply loved.

As you make your way through this book, you will quickly see a pattern of shared life experiences around a table including food, drinks, coffee, pie (there must be pie!) conversations, laughter, and memories; lots of memories.

Many of my fondest recollections are not just enjoying food around the table, but just like the little boy standing on the stool, I have always enjoyed the process of making food, learning how it all comes together, and being in the kitchen. Even better is to make food for people I care about and then spending time with them, around a table and enjoying the food I've prepared. For the holidays or summer gatherings, I sometimes start preparing the ingredients days in advance (just like my Mom, Betty, would do every holiday). The thing that brings me the most joy is the focused, intentional time together over the meal that connects us in ways that nothing else can. There's just something about breaking bread together and talking to each other without distractions. In my humble opinion, we as a people, need to rediscover and once again treasure the beautiful and simple gifts of presence, and giving others our undivided attention.

In the house where I grew up, the kitchen was the physical center of our home and family life in many ways. It was where I would spend the most time with my mom, learning and listening to her as she prepared food for our family or for a gathering of hungry teenagers during our high school and college years. Our house was a frequent spot for gatherings of friends and my mom would prepare pizzas, or tacos, and a dozen or more kids would show up to partake. I remember always loving that my friends loved to come to our house and loved my mom and dad.

Other times at home, perhaps after school or on a weekend, I would sit at the kitchen table with just me and Mom talking about our day. I am certain I honed my inquisitive, conversational skills early on around that table and many others since. It was also where our family of four boys, with mom and dad, spent countless hours sharing meals nearly every day of our lives growing up. By the time I came along, my Dad had his own construction and millwork business located within walking distance of our home out in the country, so he would usually walk home for lunch. We would eat together around that same table during the summer when school was out and I was home, with the older brothers sometimes working with Dad at his business during the day.

Being the youngest of four sons, I recall how much I loved those times of connection and being together with Mom and Dad and my three older brothers, Rick, Gary, and Kevin. Yes, there were occasional skirmishes and sarcastic words between brothers, a spilled drink or *much-needed* lessons in manners and table etiquette usually from Dad, but most of my memories from around the table are filled with love, laughter, delicious food and conversations.

With my brothers being a bit older than me (6, 9, and 12 when I was born), there were several years during elementary school, junior high, and high school when my brothers were away most of the time for their school activities, and later college and graduate school. Because of that, I had many afternoons after school at home with just Mom and me. In fact, by the beginning of my 8th grade year, all three of my brothers had left home and I mostly lived as an *only child* from then on (except for holidays and occasional summer visits from my brothers and later their wives). That reality was both a blessing and a point of sadness in my life. It was a joy to have so much focused individual time at home growing up with Mom and Dad. But the departures of my brothers always left an emptiness inside, when they would leave for college (often gone months at a time) or to their post-college and career lives, states away. Because of the age differences and their attending college and graduate school in Kansas and Ohio, and then taking jobs in Iowa, Kansas, and Missouri, those times together in Indiana during my adolescence were cherished but limited.

Starting my fourth-grade school year, Mom started working a part-time job, six days a week as a breakfast cook at the Zeta Beta Tau fraternity at Indiana University in Bloomington. With two sons in college at that time, I'm sure our middle-class family needed all the extra income we could get. So, Mom would get up early in the morning and leave by 6am before I woke up for school and started making 7am breakfast for 45-50 sleepy college students. Because it was a part-time job, mom was able to negotiate starting at 7am and leaving about 2pm each afternoon arriving home by the time I was off the school bus a little after 3pm. After cooking most of the day for the men of ZBT, she would drive the half-hour home and before long the yellow school bus was stopping at the front of our house on Upper Schooner Valley

Road. Arriving home from school I would burst through the door and quickly land in the kitchen with my Mom.

As I would spend those late afternoons in the kitchen, I would ask Mom many questions about a lot of things, but as she would start working on dinner, I would usually wander over and ask what she was making. She welcomed my questions and curiosity and would say "come here and I'll show you". I didn't have to stand on a stool anymore and would watch and learn from her in the kitchen, often helping to make (and sample!) some of my favorites. I'm sure I didn't fully realize it then, but I equated that time in the kitchen with having Mom's attention, being close to her, and learning about what she was doing. It was also a time of feeling loved, feeling like I wasn't a bother, feeling connected.

Mom's informal cooking lessons continued as I grew into a teenager, and college student, yet my interest in learning new recipes, and making food with Mom did not wane. After I graduated from college, I spent a year living back at home, and working between college and graduate school to save up for the lean graduate school years. I recall one day I said to Mom that when I moved off to attend Ball State University for graduate school, that I wanted to know how to make my favorite foods, especially her crispy fried chicken cooked in the ever-popular black iron skillet. She said "Well, let's plan to have you make a meal once a week before you move." And that is what we did.

Most weeks that year, she taught me to make a meal with a different recipe and she and Dad would even eat it! As she was showing me the steps, I would take notes and write down the recipes for each item. To this day, one of my most precious possessions is a tattered yellow spiral-bound notebook, that became *The Betty Cookbook* of meals she taught me how to make during my last year at home in Brown County.

Red Door Restaurant

Another place where it was common to enjoy homemade food, and time with family around a table, was at the Red Door Restaurant. My grandma, Edna (Powell) Williamson, operated the restaurant in the middle of my hometown of Nashville, Indiana from the late 1950's to the mid-1990's when she retired at the young age of 82. The Red Door Restaurant was a local favorite on the main street through our one stoplight town, and another place in my life that felt like a home base where I was welcomed and loved. If I had after school programs, ballgames or practices, the Red Door was close enough to my school that I could walk over and know that someone from my extended family would be there. Either my Grandma Edna (MaMa to us), my Grandpa Paul Williamson (PaPa), an aunt, uncle, or cousin would be there (sometimes all of the above!) and my MaMa would always say "do you want something to eat"? Of course, the answer was always an enthusiastic YES!

The Red Door Restaurant offered a warm welcome and southern-style, East Kentucky home-cooked, comfort food. MaMa Edna was born near Mount Sterling, Kentucky and she made what I would call "home food" at the Red Door. Early each morning around 5:30am, she would leave their house up on the hill across from the house where I grew up, and drive to the Red Door to start the coffee, bake pies, and cobblers all before opening at 7am for breakfast. Her pies and fruit cobblers were legendary, especially her Sugar Cream Pie. My favorite was usually blackberry or peach cobbler with a scoop of vanilla ice cream. Most days you would have to arrive early enough in the day, or your favorite pie or cobbler might just be sold-out.

Most of the employees at the Red Door were cousins, grandchildren, aunts, and uncles and friends who became family. Years before MaMa opened the Red Door, her mother and my Great Grandma, Miriam Warmouth Powell, had operated a restaurant called The Gables Café on the very same block of our hometown just a couple of doors south of where the Red Door used to be. "Mom Powell" was always how my family referred to her. Sadly, she passed away before I was old enough to ever know her, but I treasure my family stories and her legacy lives on in all of us.

One of my most treasured possessions is a stainless-steel milkshake machine that my parents had in our kitchen growing up. I made way too many milkshakes with that machine, but at the time had no idea the history of it. Only years later, did I discover that it had been from The Gables. I had asked my dad one time, about where it had come from, and he told me that he could remember the milk shake machine sitting on the counter at The Gables in the early 1940's when he was just a young teenager. And it still works now over eighty years later!

So, you can see that food, family and connections run deep in my clan and my love for local cafes, gathering places, and unique hometown spots is truly a generational legacy. I guess you could say it's in my DNA; sharing food, coffee and conversation is a part of my love language!

I think some of these early memories and stories from my child-hood relate to why I took to the road in 2021 and into 2022, traveling widely and visiting dozens of cities, and over 60 cafes in 15 states on what I simply called *The Coffee Tour*. As I made my way from state to state, town to town, café to café, I would post pictures and updates on social media to keep interested friends and family informed of my latest adventures and whereabouts. Having transitioned from a long career in higher education, and now working for myself as an executive coach and consultant, the newfound flexibility and freedom to travel was a needed balm for what had taken place the two years prior. More to come on that but suffice to say my mental and emotional "bucket" was nearly empty by that summer of 2021 and much in need of healing, and to somehow try and find joy again. I was hoping it might be something I could rediscover rolling across states and towns, testing out local coffee shops and cafes, meeting interesting people, and having time to reevaluate my life journey and what I wanted the next years to look like.

In the pages that follow, I not only describe unique and interest-ing towns and places, but take a deeper look at why places, people and life-giving interactions are so dear to me and to others I met in towns across the United States.

Sometimes I wonder if we have lost some of these precious things like a sense of community, connection, or the ability to look at each other and talk over coffee or a meal without a mobile device buzzing for our attention. I believe a part of joy is also having *a sense of place*, or home and belonging. My journey of two years across the states has affirmed to me that those people and places do still exist, and we can have a renewed joy and sense of being where we belong — no matter where home is really.

It may be that we need to be more intentional about rediscovering them, and offering them to others that cross our paths, but in the dozens of towns and cafés I visited, and with those I talked to and interviewed, there is cause for hope despite everything. Community, connection and belonging are real, and we all need them in our lives whether we know it or not.

As many towns are recovering, renewing and revitalizing their downtowns, perhaps along with the physical restorations, we can rediscover the intangible joys that people felt who once lived and shopped there in years past? I believe we can, but I need you to come with me on the journey and rediscover the countless places and relationships that need to be rejuvenated, renewed, or restored. We are doing that in my town, and you can do that in *your* town, on the streets where you live, in the neighborhoods where you drive and walk, and *your* favorite local cafés and coffee shops. Of course, there are many other places to help make that happen, but my journey was primarily focused on coffee shops and cafés that reminded me what it felt like to be that little boy standing on a stool in the kitchen making cheeseburgers.

As I visited the many cafés, I not only felt a joyful connection in many of those places, but also back to my Brown County home in Indiana, my family and friends, my past, growing up, cooking, hospitality, Schooner Valley and the Red Door.

Though I didn't fully recognize it during my travels, I realized later that I was also running from the grief and sadness of having lost my Dad in March of 2021 and my Mom in May of 2019, just 22 months apart. No matter their ages, or how long we had them in our lives (Dad was 92; Mom was 89) the death of both my parents that close together, brought a painful sense of loss and a vast emptiness inside me in a space that had been filled for so many years by the two people in the world who loved me the most.

So, a few months after losing my Dad, I packed a few things, piled them in my 2010 Hyundai and mapped out my journey to coffee shops, cafés and restaurants near and far. In the pages that follow, I'll share what I found there, and even more importantly what I found in me.

Part 1
The World Changed

As the first wave of the pandemic in the spring of 2020 started hitting the United States, the spread of COVID-19 resulted in orders from state and federal government, to shelter at home, not gather in public places, and avoid contact with other people in an effort to slow the spread of the deadly virus. Schools and universities went on extended spring breaks that March, that then led to schools and campuses closing for the rest of the semester and seemingly overnight, moving to virtual learning on various video platforms. We were going to "flatten the curve" of rising cases and deaths and then get back to our lives...we thought.

Because that spring 2020 semester was no longer taking place in-person, high schools and colleges were forced to cancel traditional graduation ceremonies and celebrations. For most of the 2020 graduates, and many more in 2021, what they had looked forward to for years, walking across a stage and graduating, was simply wiped out or held online or in drive-up style in a parking lot. My youngest daughter's college graduation was one of the casualties and her graduation was celebrated in my son's backyard, with Pomp & Circumstance playing on my phone. She wore her cap and gown, and her brother stood in for the university president, and congratulated her while we filmed the moment on our phones. It was a sad substitute for a life event that couldn't be recovered or experienced later, yet thousands of other families did something similar for their graduates and tried to make the best of it. Many families held gatherings that were much more painful and tragic due to the loss of a loved one, where few could attend funeral services to support the family and honor the loved one who had passed. It was a new low for most all of us.

Looking back on that period, the many months of quarantine, illness, and loss after loss, the toll on communities, families and students is still playing out in ways beyond the scope of this project. The damaging impact on mental health, learning and education, teachers, and student learning is still unfolding. Losses are still being calculated and reflected in declines in student learning and a major teacher shortage across the U.S. due to the stress and burnout they have experienced. Needless to say, the cumulative damage and costs are many, likely beyond calculation. This kind of devastating impact has played out across industries besides education as well as communities around the globe.

Restaurants, cafés, and most businesses had to close or drastically alter the delivery of products and services during 2020 and 2021. For months at a time, many food establishments could only offer online or phone-ahead ordering and curb pick-up services if they were able to be open at all. Restaurant and bar employees by the thousands were *suddenly* unemployed due to the forced closure of their places of employment. Besides the devastating overall impact that we have witnessed, people lost wages, and family members and their very livelihoods were at stake. Sadly, many places of business, non-profits, and ministries simply did not survive the financial impact and closed forever.

After the initial surge of the global pandemic in 2020, there was a period months later where an initial downturn in the number of cases allowed the return of a limited amount of dine-in service at cafés and restaurants. Initially, most places (at least where I live) were allowed to use 25% of their seating and customers had to sit far apart due to social distancing guidelines. Of course, we know now that the initial surge was just one of many that the world and the United States would experience.

Prior to the global explosion of COVID-19, I had decided to conclude my tenure working full-time in higher education and had started building my executive coaching, training, and people development business. During the time we could gather once again in public, I invited two dear friends, Sarah, and Staci, to meet me for coffee. We gathered at our favorite coffee place and with me scaling up my business, I wanted to glean their ideas and feedback. They are both strong, gifted leaders, who bring a spectrum of insights and experience to the business community. I knew they would have many helpful ideas and suggestions for growing my business. At the time, Sarah was serving as the CEO of an area Chamber of Commerce, and Staci was the Executive Director of the Convention & Visitors Bureau for the area where we live. I wanted to ask them questions, test my ideas and content, planned scope of services, key connections, and needs for people development in our region.

What was intended to be a one-hour business-related conversation turned into two hours of deep conversation between friends. The initial discussion related to business interests and their advice for my growing full-time venture. However, our conversation quickly arrived at a deeper realization of *how much* we had missed the opportunity to simply be together, see friends and family in-person, and connect with others in our community. At the end of our time together, we almost hated to leave, and Staci said "This just brought me so much JOY!" It had been a long time since most of us had felt the joy of being together and that word struck a chord deep in my soul.

We decided right then, to begin meeting every month or so to talk, listen, learn and connect with each other and to do so at different area cafés. For an extroverted connector like me, that sounded like a perfect balm after months of online video meetings in my basement, and state mandated stay-at-home life.

Our thought was that we could visit and support a variety of local places fighting for their financial lives, encourage them, provide some business and revenue, and as much as we could, just *see* people in the community and enjoy being together as friends. I jokingly started calling our area outings *The Coffee Tour*.

What started as three friends meeting at *Stefari Café* in Kankakee, Illinois, led me to begin thinking about not only visiting local coffee shops and cafés, but to experience a more extended *Coffee Tour* in dozens of towns and states. In a number of ways, for me the idea felt like a "comeback tour" of connection after a lengthy period of loneliness and social isolation.

I figured if I could see many of those local cafes, villages and towns, and share the journey on social media, maybe a few more people would venture out and safely visit those places near them, and help "keep the lights on" in their hometown.

Not long after that, I was sitting at a table at Stefari and casually posted a picture of my table and a beautiful latte, giving a shout-out on their behalf. In that post, I simply asked people "What are your favorite local coffee places?" The likes, comments and shares started to come in quickly, and before I knew it, I had over 30 local cafes suggested to me from all over the U.S. for cafés in Las Vegas, Colorado, Atlanta, Philadelphia, and New York. I thought "Wow! Maybe I'm on to something?" More than two years later, the list continues to grow and there are countless local cafés and restaurants in other states that I haven't been to yet. From that post on social media, it felt like I had "hit a chord," so to speak. And people were excited to share their favorite café but also celebrate the opportunities to gather again and support small businesses in their hometowns.

Soon, *The Coffee Tour* idea began to take root, and as I hit the road that summer and posted pictures and favorite coffees from my stops on social media, more suggestions would come in. I had decided to not only visit as many places as possible, making personal visits to coffee shops and cafés, but also doing occasional interviews with some of the founders and owners, and learning the history and stories of their cafés. The experience revealed a fascinating, eclectic mix of places with shared traits, yet each one was beautifully unique and different.

Along the way, there were rich, personal conversations with owners and local customers about what makes their favorite place special and brings joy to those who come there, work there, and *together* create community, a sense of place; and a place *to belong*.

Between July 2021 to the end of 2022, I visited over 60 unique, locally owned coffee shops and cafés in 15 states. What follows is a glimpse into my journey seeing first-hand how coffee shop and café owners and the people they serve, continue coming together, creating community, connection and belonging. I would later understand that the journey allowed me to explore much more than just good food, warm hospitality and coffees. It enabled me to begin processing and facing some transitions, losses and sadness that had saturated my life the previous few years.

Many of you will be able to relate to my journey from your personal experiences of transitions, loss and sadness. In my worst moments, I sometimes wondered "Will I ever *really* be happy again, and have joy in my life"? As I climbed in my Hyundai and started *The Coffee Tour*, I really wasn't sure what the answer to that question would be. To be honest, I doubted whether the answer would be yes.

More Than Just Coffee

When I first started visiting coffee shops, and connecting with people, the one word that stayed at the center of my thoughts was what Staci had said; *joy*. My initial point of *The Coffee Tour* was to simply see the many unique corner cafés, mom-and-pop shops, repurposed and restored historic buildings in as many towns as possible.

I saw many towns like Hannibal, Missouri, St. Charles, Missouri and Bentonville, Arkansas that have revitalized their downtown areas, offering a sense of place, and *places to be.* Other towns that I visited are in the earlier stages of reviving those beautiful, historic places and their city centers in the process. A key factor in town, after town, was almost always a group of small businesses taking a chance, betting on themselves and their community, to renew spaces in their downtowns that most corporations long ago abandoned for big-box facilities on the edge of town. There are a few exceptions, but typically, it has been local businesses and non-profits, local needs, and local people doing the hard work to renew, rebuild, and revitalize the places where they live, shop and gather.

In every case, it takes people with passion and creativity to be reminded of what their town once was, what it can be again, and how to renew and revitalize their community in new and exciting ways. Seeing these many examples in town after town encouraged me and inspired me to drive to the next town and to also help that happen where I now live.

The renewal and revitalization of local towns is something I love and care about for many reasons. Having grown up in the small village of Nashville, Indiana that was founded in 1836 as an artist's colony[i], the history is rich, and the village has over 125 shops and galleries filled with the work of artisans, crafters, painters, builders, and entrepreneurs. Nashville, Indiana is the county seat of Brown County, a popular tourist area due to beautiful, wooded hills, parks, and rivers as well as the village itself. I treasure my growing up experiences in that place I call *My Forever Home*, and the countless forms of beauty that can be created in a small community.

A New Chapter

Besides my love of small towns, and the creative gifts they hold, I also was in a time of transition in both my work and personal life. After spending three decades in higher education as an administrator and professor, I loved the learning process and the students there, yet wanted to express my love of learning in a new and different context. As a professor of organizational leadership for over eight years, followed by a decade in corporate engagement work, I increasingly had the opportunity to consult, coach, conduct trainings and retreats with companies and non-profit organizations. I had decided in 2019, that soon I would scale my fledgling people development business to be my central work focus. I started the business in 2017 and eventually planned to transition from higher education as a full-time assignment but continue teaching some on a part-time basis. For a variety of reasons, that time had come in 2020; and in the summer of 2021 I decided *The Coffee Tour* was going to be my first road trip as a solo entrepreneur, turning the page to a new chapter, exploring other places, and figuring out what my life was going to look like down the road.

It was just a couple of months prior to beginning my exit from higher education, that my dad had passed away unexpectedly in late-March 2021. It was just four months after losing my dad that I started my Coffee Tour road trip, and my heart was hurting to say the least. Losing my dad just 22 months after saying goodbye to my sweet mom in 2019 was almost more than I could bear. Dad was a steady, quiet, gentle giant to me, and I was always proud to be his son. My mom was the ever-present encourager, believer, listener, a rock of faith in our family.

Though I didn't recognize it at the time, I think I was looking for more than just unique coffee shops. I was seeking a renewed joy and adventure in new places, but I was also running from my own grief, and sadness and the suffocating sense of loss and emptiness that I was feeling. I was close to both of my parents, and the aching vacancy that their passing had created left a void that I imagine will always be there. Despite that, I was hopeful that in time the pain would lessen, that life would eventually be good again, and that I would adjust to our very different family dynamic without Mom and Dad, and perhaps maybe even find joy again. But how?

As *The Coffee Tour* started in 2021, and continued into 2022, I traveled to many states, stopped to see friends and former students, interviewed, and listened to coffee shop owners and customers. Listening to their stories, their histories, I continued to maintain my personal focus on joy, and considered where to find it, and just how I might experience it again. I wish I could tell you that it was a short journey with easy answers, but I think you know better than that. In the pages that follow, I'll revisit that journey and share some signposts that started to emerge for me.

This two-year journey was, at times, a struggle, a crawl even, because of my grief. But it was also filled with gifts like meeting new friends, reconnecting with friends I've known a lifetime, plus a wedding for one of our children, and the birth of our first grandchild. While I don't suggest that I have joy all figured out, or that what brings me joy will be your personal "recipe," but the ones that resonated with me then (and now) will be shared in the coming sections of this story. Those themes that now mean even more to me after dozens of cafes, hundreds of miles, dozens of towns, and many lonely hours in the car, are things I think I already knew from the beginning of my journey back in the hills of southern Indiana. Sometimes we must find ways to remind ourselves who we are and where our joy comes from.

As you can imagine, besides infusing caffeine from over 60 cafes and coffee shops across America, and making new friends in most places, I have also researched many books and articles on joy, happiness, thriving, meaning, belonging and purpose. My research was not just to enhance my writing, but to discover new and creative ways to grow, and heal, and perhaps figure out what joy could look like for me going forward.

Joy is something I think we all seek and hope for in our lives, yet it is not easily found or experienced often enough. In some ways, joy can seem fleeting, momentary, or temporary. The picture of a giggling little child meeting a puppy, swinging, running barefoot in the grass, or chasing bubbles at the city park seems like pure joy. Watching a child playing baseball, softball or soccer and getting their first hit, their first home run, their first goal, looks a lot like joy to me. Those moments of celebration, and the beautiful look on their face that says, "I DID IT!"

Sometimes my travels include flying, and I enjoy watching parents and grandparents at an airport welcoming their children or grandchildren home for a long-awaited visit. Hearing their shouts of "Mommy!" or "Daddy!" as they run with arms open for that welcome-home hug is priceless. During my college days, the expression on my mom's face when I came home and walked in the door of our house, was always received in a sweet, higher pitched voice "Hi Jeeefff!"

(We tend to draw out names where I come from). Late in her life when Mom would see me walking into her nursing home, I would be welcomed with that same sweet voice even if it was a bit weaker, "Hi Jeeefff!" ... *I will never forget that.*

Yes, joy can be fleeting or momentary but at the same time I believe that we can provide others (and ourselves) with frequent doses of joy as adults. Besides the occurrences of joy, it is somewhat different than happiness which is thought to be more enduring but perhaps just as elusive as joy. Joy is *related* to happiness, but the two are not synonymous. Brene´ Brown (2021) states that "joy is sudden, unexpected, short-lasting, and high intensity. It's characterized by a connection with others, with God, nature, or the universe. Joy expands our thinking and attention, and fills us with a sense of freedom and abandon"[ii]

I know many friends and family who especially feel joyful when they can be outside, perhaps in the woods, on or near a lake or river. Dar Williams (2017) describes places like this in smaller communities as having "positive proximity"[iii] which she has observed through her travels as an accomplished musician performing in small towns and communities across America.

My Dad understood the concept of positive proximity, and for him it meant we were near lakes, rivers, streams, and ponds where we would boat, fish and ski on many vacations and family trips. When possible, the cabin or campsite was *right on the water* where the sounds of the water, breezes, birds and frogs could be heard. Our family vacations rarely involved destinations that did not include large bodies of water. A popular area for our family was the many lakes and rivers located in the Ozarks region of Missouri and Arkansas. Lake of the Ozarks, Bull Shoals Lake, Table Rock Lake, and Eureka Springs were all vacation destinations for the Williamson clan back then.

As I read about positive proximity, it made sense to me that when we experience joy in certain places, like our hometowns, the house we grew up in or rivers, lakes, and mountains where we spent time on family vacations, we often attach memories and emotions to the people with whom we shared those places. Whether it was a senior trip with three of my best friends in high school to drive all night from Indiana to the Florida coast for spring break, or my recent cross country trip to visit coffee shops and cafes, we can reflect on a next chapter of life, celebrate an important birthday, or start to clear our heads or let go of things as we drive across the miles to places we have never been or return to happy places we have been many times before.

I think that was part of why my local coffee tour became a more extended, 18-month journey of growth for me. As I drove from town to town, I was often thinking about the people and places where I had experienced joy in the past and was hoping to reclaim some of the joy that had slowly, painfully leaked out of my life. It seems no accident that many of the states and places I visited or passed through on the first several months of *The Coffee Tour*, were once routes and vacation stops for my family when I was a child. I didn't think about it so much at first, I was simply following a route toward Northern Arkansas to visit a lifelong friend I met in college. For the long drive, I decided to break up the trip, and stop in different places, based on the cities or towns where other friends and former students lived. More coffee shops and cafés, connecting with friends; it all added to what turned out to be a part of my healing journey and my renewed search for joy.

Though I didn't process all of it then, I can now see the connection between joy, and spending time in some of the many happy places I had been to years ago.

There were times as I drove alone over those months, that I processed some of my grief, shed a lot of tears, sang along with the radio, and revisited some of my deepest moments of both joy and sadness. For whatever reason, it seemed like I had to go somewhere by myself for a while, to create space for my heart to heal and my happy memories to work their way to the surface of my mind.

There is truth in the phrase that "joy is the most vulnerable human emotion... The reason that is so, is because if we lose our tolerance for vulnerability, joy becomes foreboding"[iv]. In other words, if we are hesitant to seek or experience joy because we fear that it will soon leave us, then joy is foreboding. How could we bear to mostly live without joy, once we are reminded how wonderful it feels? Worse still, we forfeit the *opportunity* for joy when we push others away and refuse to risk vulnerability and the possibility of more pain. We perhaps then miss out on the joy we can only find when we do take the risk. This is not only true in our personal lives, but in our work. Research has shown that "joy is an emotional response that's vital for our well-being, cognitive functioning, and our performance at work."[v] So regardless of the location, the place, or the people, joy was and is intended to be a part of our lives and to be something we continue to find, even if it is in new and different ways and places.

So where or to whom do we go, or how do we develop or discover this sometimes-elusive experience of joy? Nicholas Epley says, "Connecting with others in meaningful ways tends to make people happier, and yet people also seem reluctant to engage in deeper and more meaningful conversation"[vi]. In other words, we long for joy but fear tends to hold us back as we wander through life looking for it. But what are we afraid of?

Is it because we fear rejection, not being taken seriously, or that we simply aren't willing to take the time to have real conversations and build deep relationships? The answers are likely different for many of us, but it seems to me that the joy we seek is at least partly found living more intentionally and deeply in community. In community we find others, and with others we can find connection. The good news is that the experience of community and connection does not have to only be found in a single destination or café, but in the people, places and things we invest in and give ourselves to. It can happen in a thousand different places in a variety of ways. For me, *The Coffee Tour* and my own journey shined a light on three key components that I examine more deeply in the following sections. Those integrated experiences that contribute to our discovery of joy are community, connection, and belonging.

Part 2
Community, Connection, and Belonging

I define joy as an intense feeling of deep spiritual connection, pleasure, and appreciation-Brene Brown.[vii]

When I started *The Coffee Tour* the spring of 2021 and into the summer, all I really knew was that I needed to take a break from all I had been through and was facing at the time, to have a change of scenery, and to meet up with friends along the way, and maybe even make some new friends as well.

Over the weeks and months that followed, with visits to dozens of quaint, cozy, local cafés and coffee shops, what I experienced were some realizations of both commonalities and differences. Unique places and owners, who had carved out a place of welcome and hospitality in their local villages and towns, but also were providing for their families, making a living, and uplifting their communities at the same time.

Section 1-Community

Roots

The Daily Grind opened in 1977 in my hometown of Nashville, Indiana. It has had multiple owners over the years but is still operating in the same location under the same name. I can recall going there with my high school friends, listening to music in a cozy dining room, with a guitarist playing in front of the native stone fireplace that still graces the café. In those early days, it wasn't so much a coffee shop as it was an eclectic café with a little bit of a cool hippy-vibe (it *was* the 70's) and served coffee, teas, sodas and a few food options. Through various iterations and owners, it has always continued to be a joy for me to stop in during many trips home to Brown County. I have roots and memories there, in the community and in that *particular* place.

Coming back home from time to time, it was a wonderful place to walk in, revisit many of those days gone by, and yet feel very much at home. In later years after I left home for college, a couple, Hal and Karis Johnson, transitioned the café to a serious coffee shop with varieties of whole bean coffee grown and roasted from all over the world. Besides my high school and college memories from the late-70's and early 80's, the Daily Grind was the only *true* coffee shop in my hometown and continued to be so for over 25 years. Hal stood ready at the front counter every time I was there. He was a gregarious, friendly guy who seemed to know everyone. Each time I walked in there, he would smile and say, "Hey, buddy!" even though it might have been a year or two since my last visit. I have a feeling he said that to everyone, because it makes you feel welcome without Hal having to remember all those names. Since I came in every chance I got, I had told him previously, that I was a hometown Brown County native who had lots of good memories at the Daily Grind even before they owned it, and many more during their tenure. Hal was and still is, the biggest Green Bay Packer fan I have ever known. I don't think I ever saw him that he didn't have his weathered Packers hat on. The vibe during those years leaned heavily on his love for the Packers, but it didn't overwhelm the place. It just added the right spice and hometown flavor to the hearty welcome each time I walked in.

Several years ago around 2008, when Hal and Karis still owned the café, two of my children and I were in town and met my sixth-grade teacher, Mary Kilgore, for coffee at The Daily Grind. She regaled them with stories about elementary school Jeff. I had to wince every once in a while, listening to the stories (I was 12 once upon a time!), but so much joy at seeing a dear friend and mentor connecting with my own children in that same place and passing down those stories. Mary was a teacher who demanded excellence, and she saw something in me before I could see or believe it myself. Having roots in places that are a part of our story can be so powerful for remembering who we are, where we came from, and what it feels like to live in community and have roots.

Hal and Karis have since retired and sold the café in 2018 to another couple Andy & Denise Robison, who now own the Daily Grind. They have given it their own warmth, flavor and look, but it still remains a favorite place and holds many memories of my growing up years and the past three decades. Through the different eras, for me, nothing can compare to the Daily Grind on a chilly Saturday morning, a hot mug of coffee, the aroma of my favorite coffee beans, and my eternal roots to Brown County, my forever home.

Local

One of my first weeks of the Coffee Tour the summer of 2021 was spent in Fort Wayne, Indiana visiting over ten different coffee shops. Ahead of my visits, I researched each place, learned about their stories and arranged to talk to a few of the owners and learn more. That particular day, I had arranged to spend some time with Paul Demaree, co-owner of Firefly Coffee House located on North Anthony Boulevard. Firefly was one of the Fort Wayne places that came up frequently when I posted a survey on social media about favorite local coffee places, so I set my sights on going there.

Along with Old Crown Coffee, which is also on North Anthony Boulevard in Fort Wayne, Firefly opened in 1999 long before coffee shop culture really started to emerge in the Midwest. In fact, there were no franchised coffee shops in Fort Wayne when these two places opened their doors to local coffee lovers. Firefly and Old Crown Coffee have always been local and operate out of their original locations.

The conversation I had with Paul that July sitting in their shaded outdoor patio, was one of the initial interviews I conducted. I had arrived early that morning for my appointment, so I grabbed a coffee inside and came to the patio *incognito* to watch, listen and learn what makes this place so special. Soon, I saw a gentleman amble out to a table nearby with a beautiful wooden box under one arm, and a chess board in his other hand. He said hello to a group of men nearby (clearly *Firefly* regulars) then sat down at a table with a young man who appeared to be about 14 years old. At this point, the man placed the chess board on the table, opened the wooden box, and began to take out these lovely carved chess pieces and placed them on the board. Soon, he and the teenager were talking casually, setting up the pieces, sizing up their side of the board, and the game began. Having grown up the son of a woodworker, and playing many games of chess with my dad, I was instantly intrigued.

Between moments of quiet reflection and calculated moves, the man would ask questions. "How is your summer going?" "What is your mom up to?" "Does she still work at...?" Then he would listen to the young man... and listen...and listen. As time went on, the questions or comments from the man to the teenage boy delved a little deeper. Things like "You know, it's not easy being a single mom, working a lot of hours, trying to be a good mom". The words the gentleman spoke were encouraging, almost pastoral, but offered gentle guidance for the young man to consider. The teen was engaged, talkative, and responded to this mentor's words in a way that told me this wasn't their first conversation.

I later learned that the young man had experienced somewhat of a tough family life, and perhaps not that many people were investing in him like the mentor sitting across the chess board. This mentor, who I did not know until later, was Paul.... the co-owner of Firefly Coffee House. I sat nearby and casually observed him spending at least a half hour playing chess, but more than anything he was talking with the young man, being present, and showing him he mattered. Before long, the game wrapped up, and the group was disbursing so I wandered over and introduced myself to Paul. I had figured out during the chess game, that this was the Paul I had emailed and scheduled an interview with. I couldn't wait to learn more about his story and how he and his wife had chosen to be local and invest all their business and energies in the Fort Wayne community.

Loving fine woodworking, I was immediately drawn to the beautiful chess board and wood box that Paul had carried out earlier. It was intricate, with multiple types and colors of wood and it turned out that Paul made the whole set and is an accomplished woodworker! After I introduced myself and began to visit with him, I had a chance to closely examine the chessboard, each crafted chess piece, and the wooden box. It was done with such high-quality workmanship, put together with excellence. That is something that I admire so much in art and really all aspects of life and work. Beautiful, solid cedar, contrasting, curving grains with both the rich red color along with the lighter grains naturally integrated. This beautiful collection was one of a kind. My dad would have really enjoyed this piece of artwork and talking to Paul about his craft and designs.

After quite a conversation about woodworking, and the part it played in my dad's business, and therefore my upbringing, Paul and I began to talk more specifically about Firefly Coffee House, its history and place in the local community.

I invited Paul to tell me the story about Firefly, why they started the café, and what he loves about this cozy place that has been such a central part of their life and the community. He recounted examples of people coming to the café as visitors, becoming regulars, and then friends. The atmosphere and culture of the place is that anyone, and everyone is welcome there regardless. In a culture where appearances, politics or lifestyles can be so divisive, here was a local place that was designed to be a welcoming, gracious place of hospitality, kindness, love and acceptance.

As our conversation progressed, it was deep and real as we talked about the journey with his wife, Cyndi, and what led them to the opening of Firefly Coffee House. We talked about things he has learned along the way, what he has left behind (he was a hospital chaplain for over 10 years), what things seem to make sense in this world, and others that just don't. Paul witnessed such suffering and tragedy in his years as a hospital chaplain that it has left wounds on his heart and his faith.

It was intriguing to hear how he feels about their customers and the loving regard he has for them. It seemed the only "rule" of the house was that kindness and respect are required no matter what, no matter who, and I like that a lot.

As a child I lived in a rural area, where whippoorwills and fireflies were an almost nightly occurrence in the summertime. Hundreds of those tiny little lighted bugs drew us toward them, and I would roam around in the fields behind our house, following them to get a closer look. The best thing was when there would be hundreds of fireflies in the same area, lighting up the night. It was magical, and a source of joy that I have never outgrown. Of all the bugs that I encountered in the country growing up, I was never afraid of fireflies (we called them *lightning bugs*). Besides giving light, they always seemed gentle, would land on you without fear of harm, didn't sting or bite and continued to shine a light wherever they were. It was rare to see just one. It was more common to see them together in one place.

I think Firefly Café is doing something very similar; shining a light, attracting others, bringing people together, and inviting them to come closer without fear.

Neighborhoods

The first morning I walked into Friendly Fox, I was greeted by Morgan, the barista working that morning. She immediately smiled, said hello, and asked what she could get started for me. I walked to the counter and told her, "I'm a first timer. I haven't been here before." She asked me my name, and offered hers, immediately helping me feel seen. They weren't busy when I arrived that weekday morning, so I asked her how long she had been working there, what she liked about the place, and what her favorite drinks and foods were from the menu. She had started working there while attending college nearby, and decided to remain in the community, stay involved in dance and performing, and working at Friendly Fox. She seemed like the perfect fit for the vibe of this historic corner café, with houses in every direction. The café opened in 2007 in the historic Southwood Park neighborhood in Fort Wayne, Indiana. Their corner location was once a neighborhood drug store established in the 1950's. For a time, it was Schmidt's Pharmacy, and later Hutson Pharmacy.

Since I was going to be in the Fort Wayne area for a few days, I decided to come back to Friendly Fox the next morning and grab breakfast the second day. The main reason I did so was because it felt very welcoming and comfortable after just one visit! When I came in the door the second morning, Morgan smiled and said "Hi Jeff!" As I walked up to the counter, Morgan introduced me to one of the baristas who was not there the previous day and said "This is Jeff. He came here for the first time yesterday, but now he is a *regular!*" Is it any wonder that Fort Wayne locals come here for coffee or breakfast on their way to work, or grab lunch or dinner inside or on the lovely, covered patio out front? You are only a visitor *once*, and then you are a *regular*.

That sense of *place attachment* that Warnick described in her book, *This is Where You Belong* (2016), is key to the creation and nurturing of community[viii]. My experience at Friendly Fox was one that invites in locals as well as visitors and beckons me to return the next time I am in Fort Wayne.

After my initial week of *The Coffee Tour* in Indiana, my focus turned west to a stretch of interstate starting on I-57 near my home south of Chicago, to downstate Illinois toward Missouri, on to St. Louis, through other cities in southwest Missouri and then across Arkansas. Driving that initial stretch of southern Illinois, to the Missouri River and historic St. Charles, then on to Columbia, and Springfield, I was reminded of so many good times with my family, and summer vacations that I had once spent in many of the towns along this route during my teens and early 20's.

Our family vacations had often been to different lakes and destinations in the Ozarks region of Missouri and Arkansas. Retracing those steps and memories that Fall, held a lot of emotions and reflections of joy going back to those trips. One of the places we visited more than once was Osage Beach, Missouri and the Lake of the Ozarks. My next overnight stop on the tour was a lakefront room looking out over the beautiful lake I had visited years ago as a teen. That first visit to Lake of the Ozarks was over fifty years ago, but the memories are vivid and treasured. Visiting the lake community on my tour, included places I recalled from long ago and others that had come into being in the years since my first trip. Many of the coffee places have emerged since those early days in the 1970's and were not there when I visited originally. As I revisited the small towns and cities along my route across the Midwest, I experienced the unique shops and cafés that Dar Williams called "the spice rack of the community."[ix]

Dar Williams is a renowned folk artist, musician and songwriter who released her first album in 1990. From her years of travel and performing, she released a book entitled *What I Found in a Thousand Towns (2017).* It delightfully describes how many small towns across the United States have found ways to create what she calls *positive proximity*, on the way to experiencing community. "When people transcend the myth that proximity means conflict and invasion of privacy, they gravitate toward finding ways to integrate the talents and skills of their community members. Not only that, after people discover each other in the commons of town, more connections are made."[x] Positive proximity, according to Williams, is reflected in three patterns which are: 1) spaces that naturally maximize the number of good interactions, 2) projects that build a town's identity...helping them become *themselves*, and 3) translation; all the acts of communication that open up a town to itself and the world[xi].

For a sense of community to develop in the spaces where we live, work, and shop, Williams describes how "milling about" outside at things like farmers markets, community gardening, local sports, or even walks or hikes where there are great views (rivers, lakes, forests), as options that create proximity in positive ways.

In the context of characteristics of cafés that "increase the buzz of community-focused discussions,"[xii] Williams has identified four from her travels. First is the "two-roomer" with the main room being the counter, where the coming and going of pickup orders takes place, and perhaps a brief stint at a few tables nearby. The second room can be used for a variety of things; extended conversations, a cozy space or a quiet place to journal and destress. Second, is the "toy corner" where parents of young children tend to land and enjoy parent connections and conversations with other grown-ups (while wrangling the little ones nearby). The third aspect is the friendly staff who work in these places. They know the locals, welcome new customers, and provide hospitality and kindness to everyone. The fourth observation by Williams is that the space *reflects the community*. It can be local art, books by local authors, live music, event promotions, or general community news.

From my own travels in 2021 & 2022, a common response from the owners and staff where I visited, as to the "why" of starting their own cafés, they focused on having a gathering place for their community. The shops, from the newer ones to those that had been around over twenty years, provided unique coffees and fresh, crafted food but in addition, their venture was more about bringing local people *together* and serving them in a place *they* wanted to be themselves. I loved how the dozens of cafés were each an expression of the creativity, flavors, cultures, histories and personalities of their owners, staff, and communities. It was as if each café, each community is an in-progress mosaic and each person who comes there, and sticks around even a little while, adds to the act of creation that each place seems to be experiencing. It's almost like these places are in a process of both renewing and creating a history and a story in each particular community.

Few people open cafés and coffee shops, with the central purpose of getting rich. They want to make an honest living, provide for their families, engage their local community and be a part of something bigger than themselves. As communities offer different options for public places to gather with others; it provides each of us (and all of us), a place to be, a place to do things *together*. In every city, town or village where we gather, we live out our stories in the common, everyday realities with the people we choose to be around. The places where we gather, how we feel when we are there, and the sense of welcome we feel, is a central part of what brings us back.

One of my favorite sitcoms from the 80's and 90's was a show called "*Cheers*". It has one of the more memorable theme songs that plays at the beginning of each episode.

Making your way in the world today
Takes everything you've got
Taking a break from all your worries,
Sure would help a lot.
Wouldn't you like to get away?
Sometimes you want to go
Where everybody knows your name
And they're always glad you came.
You want to be where you can see

Troubles are all the same

You want to go where everybody knows your name.

(1982, Gary Portnoy, Judy Hart Angelo, songwriters).

It was set in a downtown Boston bar, owned by a character named Sam Malone, who was a fictitious former Red Sox pitcher (played by Ted Danson). "Sammy" seemed to know everyone, or at least treated them like a friend, as he served up something to drink. He was a master at asking questions, and showing interest in new customers (especially the ladies).

In the early days of the show, Sam was paired with *Coach*, the other bartender, who was a simple-minded, friendly older man who Sam knew from his baseball days. Coach always led the *Cheers* welcome when the daily customers, like Cliff, Norm, and Frasier came in. Along with Coach, many of the patrons at the bar would call out their names with gusto...especially "Norm!"

In later years of the shows run, the Coach character was replaced by a lovable, naïve young kid from Hanover, Indiana (a real place) named Woody (played by Woody Harrelson). Woody was a good contrast to the Boston locals with his friendly, aw-shucks Midwestern perspective on things, as well as his occasional confusion over city life and how things were done in Boston as opposed to "back in Hanover..."

I've loved the show since my college days, and a big part of that were the ways that they connected, supported each other, sometimes made fun of each other, engaged in debates and arguments, but ultimately, they cared about each other (even the grumpy barmaid, Carla) and kept showing up day-after-day.

One of the earliest realities of the pandemic and sheltering at home was the loss of gathering in places as a community. That loss of community then led to an increase in loneliness. "At the heart of loneliness is the absence of meaningful social interaction–an intimate relationship, friendships, family gatherings, or even community or work group connections."[xiii]

With that context of wanting "to go where everybody knows your name," I quickly started referring to some of the coffee places I visited, as having the *Cheers factor*. They had found a way to create a welcome space and build rapport with people who came in (daily or new) and learned some of their story in short order. The *Cheers factor* is also another way of saying there was a sense of community there; people seemed to have a place, liked coming there, liked those who did (well, mostly), and wanted to be known. I found many similarities as I traveled the country and visited dozens of coffee shops. Some had a very evident "Cheers factor" while I was there, looking, listening, and talking to owners and customers. The variety of places described in this book, had a unique way to provide their own "Cheers factor" and keep people coming back again and again.

Along the way, there were many rich conversations about their history, what makes each place unique and special in bringing *joy* to customers and friends who came there and helped create community. I'm certain there are places like that near you or in your community that I haven't visited yet. If you have found yourself desiring a renewal or even a discovery of community and the relationships that can come from engaging, then I urge you to give it a try. Because I think we all want to have those places where everybody knows our name.

Section II–Connection

Over most of 2020, and 2021, the global pandemic frequently isolated us from one another perhaps more than ever before. As the nation began reopening after the first wave, we slowly returned to public places, with limits and protocols still in place. The extent of how much, how often, or how many of us could gather and where, varied through additional surges, peaks and valleys. Thankfully, the numbers of cases and hospitalizations eventually dropped significantly, and the requirements rolled out by federal and state governments were lifted.

As our communities were able to venture out and connect since the height of the pandemic, I've noticed how many people are embracing the opportunity to come together in-person and reconnect with others in new ways. I believe we are created for community and the isolation and aloneness we experienced in 2020-2021 especially, has taken a significant toll on our levels of joy, happiness, and mental health.

Family gatherings, birthdays, anniversaries, weddings, and so many other things we used to take for granted are now even more of a cause for celebration. In one case, I know of a family who refused to have Christmas in 2021 because one of their loved ones was in critical condition, hospitalized for months due to COVID and they made up their minds they would not gather for Christmas until she was better and could join them. It wound up being May 2022 when they all headed to a lodge in Tennessee and *finally* had their long-awaited family Christmas. The joy experienced by that dear family to be able to gather, connect and renew their relationships in person, was simply immeasurable. These kinds of gatherings also returned to our communities in the hometown places where we spend most of our days when we are not in our homes. The joy of meeting friends for lunch or coffee, once taken for granted, has been progressively rediscovered and reminds us of our innate need for each other. We have renewed and rediscovered friendships, familiarity, and the power of community and connection. The lack of experienced community and being together in common places during 2020 and 2021 impacted us in ways far beyond doing without our favorite foods or brewed coffee in a sit-down atmosphere. The epidemic of loneliness that continues even now, is significant and painful and is showing up in both our personal and professional lives. Former surgeon general, Vivek Murthy, stated long before the pandemic, that "if we cannot rebuild strong, authentic social connections, we will continue to splinter apart."[xiv] It is even more critical now than it was in 2017.

Unable to gather or work in the same place for months at a time, we were forced to learn how to do life, school and work meetings on video platforms or at least try... (you're on MUTE!). While I do love many aspects of technology and how it can transport us to places around the globe, to see family, friends, or clients, I often missed *my people* and I believe a lot of you felt the same way.

While each of us enjoy different levels of "togetherness" due to legitimate personality differences, I believe we were created for community and being with others at least some of the time. The isolation and loneliness in so many lives in recent years have been devastating to say the least. While I like some peace and quiet from time to time, I find that extended times of isolation is not good for me and perhaps not for you.

The negative impact on global mental health during the pandemic and since seems to support that perspective. Most of us have a need for friendship and a sense of community in the places where we live and gather. It was that knowledge that led to my trek across 15 states to explore where and how people were making it happen. From Illinois, to all of the Great Lakes states, the Southeast U.S., Middle America, plus Northern California, I have witnessed joy and connection with people from every walk of life, coming together and enjoying fellowship and laughter, over coffee and food. Something different and special takes place when we break bread together and that reality transcends geography, culture, and traditions. "Connecting with others in meaningful ways tends to make people happier, and yet people also seem reluctant to engage in deeper and more meaningful conversation."[xv]

Our experiences of joy and happiness in the stories of our lives seem too often missing or rare at best. Perhaps it is that we have lost people or relationships that were most connected to us, or maybe we grew up in such a way that true connection was not modeled or taught to us. I believe that pretty much everyone desires connection with others in some form or another, but for many possible reasons like fear of vulnerability, wounds from broken families or relationships, pride, ego, or self-doubt, we sometimes stay behind our shields (or our screens) and hunker down alone with very little real human connection in our lives. I don't believe we were made for isolation from others, but rather community and connection. Social isolation and loneliness have negative physical effects that have been evidenced in the U.S and beyond. "Even before the COVID pandemic, government and public health officials were calling loneliness a significant health threat"[xvi].

The need for our lives to involve others and lessen loneliness has become not only an individual problem, but one that has taken on a global perspective. In Japan and the U.K. their governments have *ministers of loneliness* to help in lessening the impact and outcomes of loneliness among their citizens. Even before the pandemic, the alarming rates of suicide in Japan were at the core of these efforts. A ten-year initiative, led to a record low in suicides for Japan in 2018.[xvii] Sadly, that trend reversed during the pandemic and government efforts have been renewed and continue.

The U.K. established the Jo Cox Loneliness Commission in honor of a former parliament member who was passionate about the issue of suicide. The fourth responsibility of the Commission was to "create new community spaces...by creating new community cafés, gardens, and art spaces."[xviii] Their research indicated that in the U.K., over 9 million people identify *as always lonely or often lonely.* Worse still their results indicated that approximately 200,000 older adults had not had a conversation with a friend or relative in over a month!

A study from Brigham Young University found that the negative impact of isolation and loneliness was similar to those health risks identified by the Department of Health & Human Services such as obesity, activity levels, substance abuse, and others.[xix] Even if I were not a social person (enjoying the company of others more often than not) that would give me a good reason to find places to connect and be with others. Carl Marci, the author of *Rewired (2022),* stated in the context of mental health and well-being, that "the effects of social relationships are profound. They play a role in our perceptions of the world, our behaviors and ultimately our brain psychology...we are wired to connect."[xx]

Brene' Brown defines connection as "the energy that exists between people when they feel seen, heard, and valued; when they can give and receive without judgment; and when they derive sustenance and strength from the relationship." She goes on to add that "connection is in our neurobiology."[xxi]

With that in mind, it is perhaps as important as ever that we become more intentional to rediscover community, and connection, that can at least lessen the experience of loneliness and isolation, and therefore provide an improvement to our mental health, wellness and sense of belonging. The simple act of being together has a long-range impact that is both life-giving and even lifesaving! We are at risk of being people who are literally dying to connect with someone on a deeper, meaningful level. These deeper connections play out in many different places, and ways through families, friends, the sharing of food and drink, conversations, the telling and hearing of stories, and what has sadly become more uncommon–the expression of human kindness and hospitality. Fortunately, it can still be found in many places, including my local community, at *Stefari West Avenue* in Kankakee, Illinois.

Stefari West Avenue

I don't know about you, but I have a personal *coffee home.* Originally named Stefari Café their first five years, it is now called *Stefari West Avenue* located in Kankakee, Illinois. What I experienced at

Stefari with the owners, Stefan and Ari, and many friends before, during, and after the pandemic, was really the seed that became the idea for this book. The friend meetup described earlier with Sarah and Staci, then visiting some different local shops together in our region, eventually led to this book concept. That handful of visits for the three of us, to nearby cafés, eventually led to multiple weeklong solo coffee tours I have done over the last two years.

People who have frequented Stefari since they opened in 2017 have found delicious food, scratch recipes, in-house baked goods, and a wide selection of crafted coffees in a warm European vibe, plus a spirit of hospitality, kindness, and love. The culture and experience of the café was the vision of its husband-and-wife team, Stefan and Ari Frunze who met while working together in an upscale Chicago restaurant during Ari's undergraduate years at Columbia College in Chicago. Stefan had migrated to the United States from the Republic of Moldova, which is located in Eastern Europe, between the southwest border of Ukraine and the northeast border of Romania. He initially landed in the United States looking for a "connection to a place".[xxii] He first sought it in Utah while in college at Brigham Young University for two years, and then later moved on to Chicago because of the existence of strong Armenian, Ukrainian, and Romanian communities in the area.

In both Utah and later Chicago, Stefan was seeking a sense of community, a place of belonging. Perhaps something that was a connection to home. He not only found others in Chicago from his region of Eastern Europe, but he also found Ari who grew up in Kankakee, Illinois and studied fashion and creative writing at Columbia College. Both Stefan and Ari worked at a restaurant called *Boston Blackies* in the downtown River North area of Chicago. Their early roots in the food and hospitality industry during college were instrumental in learning the hard work, systems, professionalism, and quality service that would later become a key part of Stefari Cafe.

Ari's college years in Chicago only heightened her love of coffee and quality foods. According to Ari, Stefan was not that much of a "coffee person" at that stage but brought many recipes and experience with baked goods from his native Moldova. Together, their café and staff provide outstanding coffees, lattes, teas, baked goods, sourdough bread, paninis, salads and soups that are both delicious and unique but also good for the soul.

When I interviewed Stefan and Ari for this project in 2022, I asked them how they do it, offering food and beverages in a way that feels like love and friendship? The key they talked about was hiring and training their staff. Besides candidates having a kind, friendly spirit, the central thing they look for during an interview is a *connection*; people who relate well and "get it" when it comes to hospitality and working with co-workers, customers and the community. As much as the charm of a place can be enhanced with design, architecture, flowers and furniture, without the right people on staff, a café can be just another spot that doesn't necessarily draw us in and give us the desire to return. Creating this kind of place, where the staff and customers feel love and friendship, would be tested by the pandemic.

When many state governments ordered most businesses to shut down, and people to shelter at home, to avoid further spread of the virus, it was as if the world had stopped. Those who operated restaurants, coffee shops, and bars, were especially hard hit. Overnight, inside dining stopped and these places had to fight for their survival by shifting their food service to all carry out or delivery. Orders were now only available for call-in and curb-side pickup, and people like Stefan and Ari found themselves masked, running food and coffee out their doors to waiting cars, for months, to try and make a living and sustain their business until things were better. When I later asked them how they survived the pandemic, they talked about people and the local community of friends and fans. Their neighbors came out and *showed up* for them. Customers and friends were buying Stefari gift cards for hundreds of dollars, ordering *even more* food and coffee for takeout, and giving them cash gifts to use however they needed. The people they had so graciously served the previous years were now helping them, encouraging them, being there *for them*. When there is a sense of community and caring like this, people feel a connection with the place and people and rally around them during hard times. As Brene' Brown describes, we need connection along with love and belonging.[xxiii] To put it simply, it gives purpose and meaning to our lives.

As a result of the exceptional experience at Stefari Café in their first five years, Stefan and Ari have now opened a new, larger location just a few blocks from their original cafe. The restaurant is now called *Stefari West Avenue,* and they have brought their original warmth, ambiance and extraordinary food and drink to a different historic location in downtown Kankakee. It is a must-see venue and experience whether you are local or passing through the area, just an hour south of Chicago.

As I traveled to other cities and states and met dozens of owners like Stefan and Ari who had survived the pandemic, I found that keys of community, connection and relationships had also saved other family-owned cafés and coffee shops states away. At places like *Frontier Perk Cafe*, in St. Charles, Missouri, I met another husband-and-wife team who brought together their love of food, coffee, culture and hospitality with their unique international flair that is embedded in their story and where their stories began.

Frontier Perk Café–St. Charles, Missouri

Imagine opening your dream business in late 2019; a cozy café in a historic district with brick streets, located within walking distance of the Missouri River and blocks of other historic buildings, restaurants, cafés, shopping and businesses located nearby. It was the perfect place for John and Ashley Kroger to bring together their collective work experiences, blend their family cultures and introduce elegant food and coffee with a Central American flair, rooted in Ashley's birth country of Nicaragua.

John and Ashley launched Frontier Perk Café in the fall of 2019 and quickly drew many customers and friends, who helped them quickly grow into a favorite destination. It was that quick start and the community of customers and friends who would later stand by them and help them survive a global pandemic that hit just four months after their opening. Who could survive in that context? John and Ashley did, and Frontier Perk Café did.

My first visit to Frontier Perk came as I was on my way to Kansas to visit one of my daughters and I had intentionally built in some extra days on my *Coffee Tour* to visit places along my route. By then, we were past the initial surge of COVID and could once again gather in places like John and Ashley's. Their front seating area was understandably full and grabbing a free table was not an easy task, given the popularity of the place, the crafted food, coffee and welcoming experience that awaited me. After ordering and grabbing an open table, I let one of their staff members know I was the person who had emailed a few days prior about connecting with John and Ashley. After meeting them that day, I quickly sensed their personal warmth and gift of hospitality and connecting with people. In just a few minutes, I learned more and ended up getting a quick picture of us together and then let them get back to their work serving customers and friends. We made plans for a follow up conversation which took place several weeks later.

When I had the chance to video call John and Ashley, one of the things I wanted to learn more about was how they survived as a business after only being open four months prior to the pandemic drastically altering their lives and shutting down their business to inside dining. Countless cafés, restaurants and other places in the hospitality space sadly closed their doors and could not survive the pandemic and the government-mandated shutdowns. So, I asked them how they had done it and almost without pausing they looked at each other and said in unison, "our community". They continued and talked about making connections with customers day-after-day, who quickly became friends prior to the pandemic, and then the many ways that those people stepped up, showed up, and *refused to let them fail* after such a good start.

Like many others, the Kroger's and their reduced staff adjusted to preparing food and coffee inside, running to the curb fully masked, to masked customers waiting in their cars for takeout. It was really all they could do given the situation, and they dug in, leaned on each other and their team and held steady the best they could.

Some of the places I visited and interviewed the owners, had been in business five, ten, fifteen or even 20 years and had that longevity to connect with people and build their customer base over time. With only four months before the shutdown, Ashley and John were the only café survivors I encountered who had operated less than a year before the pandemic, let alone four months and were able to continue in operation, grow and thrive since then. In fact, in November 2023 they announced that Frontier Perk Café was moving to a larger location nearby their original café in St. Charles.

When I interviewed John and Ashley, I asked about their individual strengths and roles in the café and its success in the last three years. According to Ashley, John is the lead person in the front of the cafe while she works more behind the scenes with the kitchen team. She indicated that John is the primary "connector" and friend maker at Frontier Perk Café, though my sense is that they both contribute to those aspects.

A key I observed in any of the successful post-pandemic locations was that the personality, culture and sense of welcome and hospitality that the owners exude, must be represented in their staff and the new people they hire. Whether in small family businesses or large organizations, my belief is that culture and kindness come from the top and does not happen consistently without it being an *intentional, trained priority* from the leaders in hiring and employee selection. In this case it is the Kroger's who chose to bet on themselves and Frontier

Perk Café becoming the thriving community gathering place that it is today.

"Nothing reaches so deeply into the human personality, tugs so tightly, as relationship. Why? For one reason, it is only in the context of connection with others that our deepest needs can be met. Whether we like it or not, each of us has an unshakeable dependence on others."[xxiv]

Section III–Belonging

In our search for meaning in life, the work we do, who we serve, and where we spend our lives, it is no secret that joy involves more than just earning a paycheck and paying the bills. In Brene´ Brown's words "finding a sense of belonging in close social relationships and with our community is essential to well-being...we can't survive without one another."[xxv]

These connections happen in places. Places we like to go and be and stay for a while, and perhaps develop some sense of belonging there.

Victoria Derr conducted a study with children in northern New Mexico about their experience of *place*. She describes one 10-year-old boy who described a hill near his house as his "big mountain" adding "this is the best place!" She observed, "he knows where he comes from, he knows he has places he belongs, and this knowing seems to give him confidence, rootedness, and stability."[xxvi]

Author of *Who's Your City?* Richard Florida, divides people into three groups: the mobile, the stuck, and the rooted. He says that we tend to focus on the first two, but that we need not forget the third group-the rooted ones. "They have the means and opportunity to move, but choose to stay. Why do they choose to stay? Because they're content where they are."[xxviii] Could we possibly rediscover contentment on our journey to joy? *Contentment...* think about it! How many people do we know in our families or circle of friends who we would describe as "content"? It seems like we are more likely to be restless, anxious, longing for something else, longing for more, and generally *discontent*.

In a world that seems so focused on comparison and fitting into certain molds, one of my observations from visiting cafés and towns from California to Kansas, Arkansas, Missouri, the Great Lakes states, the Southeast in Kentucky, Tennessee, Georgia to the Florida coast, is to connect your unique, local heritage and history into *the stories of today.* Rather than seeking sameness and practicing imitation of the latest box store to come to town, instead discover more of the unique local history (good and bad), where they came from, who those people were, the cultures and stories that were transported to that region from somewhere else. According to Williams, "every town has its own culture, natural features, and history."[xxix] Yes, there are common denominators in countless towns (like great varieties of coffee!) but at the same time, these very differences are the creative beauty we can potentially find in so many people and places. It was how Williams described local coffee shops and cafes as the "spice rack of the community" and asked, "how do you reach into the past to find your present and future?"[xxx] In my humble opinion, we do so by bringing the stories and unique flavors from the past, into the here and now, and integrating them into our lives and experiences in ways that shape the future.

Some of the beautiful ways I have seen this happen as I traveled many a mile, was in the architecture, murals, signs, and interactions in each community. I've always been a curious person, so I like asking locals about the places and things that are unique and wonderful about their town, or neighborhood. Each one has a story.

There is a unique beauty in the process of seeing the joy and pride of the renewal and revitalization of a town's old buildings, streets, and trails while also "delving into their social history to locate themselves in the present... and growing from its roots." [xxxi]

Williams described identity building in communities related to positive proximity (stated previously). She quotes a friend who said "flowers are neutral" referring to a community beautification project in the Catskill region of New York. She states, "When there is a project afoot, even out on the bumpiest social surfaces, citizens can leave their houses...often pushing past the known frontiers into new relationships and challenges."[xxxii]

One of the stops on Dar's music tour included a place in Carrboro, North Carolina called the *Open Eye Café.* Isn't that a great name for a coffee place? She describes it as having "all the markings of a good, positive-proximity building café: lots of tables and off-to-the-side corners...a friendly staff, and a big bulletin board."[xxxiii] Their roaster states "Coffee unites the world" and he "wants to live in a place where his coffee could be a bridge to other cultures."

Along with the places and spaces where we gather, there is the reality of how we feel when we are in those historic buildings, cafés, or galleries. There is the importance of experiencing a spirit of hospitality, kindness and feeling welcomed. "Any discussion of belonging has to start with acknowledging that love and belonging are irreducible needs for all people."[xxxiv]

In my *Coffee Tour* journeys, I always looked for, listened, and observed how much I could perceive a sense of place and belonging in those many cafés. In some places like the Friendly Fox Café in Fort Wayne, I felt a sense of belonging and welcome right away and that was mostly because of the people there. Along with the engagement and welcome from staff at the places I stopped, it was also impacted by the space that was fashioned and available in each spot. Was the environment designed for staying, or for dashing in to grab your favorite beverage and then head out for the day? Some places that I visited had drive-up windows while others did not. In some places the physical location did not accommodate the drive-up option, but other owners told me they *intentionally* picked out places and buildings that did *not* have drive-up space because the experience and culture they wanted to create in their café was *a place of being* rather than a place offering a brief transaction with customers. While I sometimes hit a drive-up shop when I am traveling or have limited time, I mostly select the places that have space designed for being and lingering. Why is that? For me, having coffee is not something I prefer to do quickly or alone. Whether I am meeting a friend or client, or arriving alone, I want to make time and space in my day and my life, for moments of pause, even for a few minutes, to metaphorically get off the "treadmill" that life can feel like. Our rushed existence does not enhance our mental outlook or our overall health and wellness. Places that are located with views of a river, lake, or hills can be a respite in the middle of the day. Sidewalk seating near a bustling downtown historic district that has been renewed can bring people and events away from the interstate exits and are more the places I want to be and linger. I have often said to my students, family and friends that "relationships are everything" while exhorting them to invest in connections that are deeper and more connected than what might be the norm.

In 1938 a study began at Harvard University called the *Harvard Study of Adult Development.* The original researchers started tracking the lives of young adults that have now spanned three generations, an original group of over 700 participants, and more than 1300 descendants to date. "It is the longest in-depth longitudinal study of human life ever done." [xxxv] Their aim has been to determine what factors impact meaning, happiness, and human well-being; what they call "the good life." While we might guess that wealth, power, prestige, position, comfort, accomplishments, and other things might be the most important keys to happiness and the good life, they are not. Instead, they state that "people who are more connected to family, to friends, to community, are happier and physically healthier than people who are less well connected." [xxxvi] Relationships *are* everything! As Reuben Welch said in his 1973 classic book "we really do need each other!" [xxxvii]

For our relationships to be more than an occasional, transactional exchange, and for those places we gather to be more than just brick and mortar, the food or coffee we buy, we tend to return or stay a while, at places that give us some sense of welcome, perhaps even a sense of belonging. I am always interested in having a refill of that.

So, if we develop a sense of community, and connection in the places where we gather, is it just repeated visits that create a sense of belonging? Perhaps that is a part of it, but I believe it is more than that. Certainly, a central part of the equation is the people we see, meet, then see again. Is seeing, observing and coming in enough that the server might know our favorite drink or meal a key to belonging? That's a good start, but getting beyond this and having a sense of belonging requires us to perhaps do some internal work and take action so that we are not frequent *strangers*, but instead people who help others feel like they are seen and belong as well? Perhaps what we are ultimately looking for is to *feel loved?* Even better would be if we feel loved in the places we go, and also be willing to engage others in a way that *they* feel love from us. But what would that look like? It certainly isn't one-size-fits-all, but I do believe there are some keys that can help us develop a sense of belonging.

One of the keys to building relationships is to know more of the stories of others around us. Story is powerful for establishing our sense of identity and being known somewhere. Through ongoing conversation in common places, we have the opportunity to show interest in others, and ask a few things about them. "Do you have family around here"? is one of my favorites, because it gives me a sense of whether they are new to the community or if they have lived here most of their lives.

Naturally, I find that conversation and storytelling tend to happen in the places we go repeatedly. I love to know the names of servers at my favorite cafés, and I want them to know me too. If I don't come in for a few days, I will often get comments like "where have you been?" "We were wondering about you!" and those simple questions help me feel known and yes, even loved. For me, that is essential. Do we feel like we belong in places where we do not feel some measure of love and caring? I think not.

"True belonging doesn't require us to change who we are; it requires us to be who we are... Belonging is a practice that requires us to be vulnerable, get uncomfortable, and learn how to be present with people without sacrificing who we are."[xxxviii] In other words, belonging can take place when our focus is not so much internal (It's about ME!) but instead when our focus is on others. Are others flawed, sometimes wounded, defensive, confounding, and complex? Well, yes, but so am I. At the same time, as we learn more of each other's stories (even long-time friends) we are more likely to offer grace and tell the truth about ourselves. Also, we often find that others have some of the same insecurities, doubts, hopes and dreams as we do.

I once foolishly thought that to be accepted, or to be successful in this world, I had to act a certain way, look a certain way, and fit a mold for where I wanted to be. Later, after falling short of my own aspirations, I began to realize that the highest level of satisfaction and true success in life was for me to become the most amazing ME I could be and bring my own unique spirit, gifts, personality, *and* flaws to the world in such a way, that I helped others to be *their* best selves. In other words, helping them feel they have permission to be unique (if even a little weird!) while not risking outright rejection or ridicule for not fitting someone else's mold or making others comfortable in their attempts at being an imitation. If Brene Brown is correct (and I believe she is) when she says "authenticity is a requirement for belonging"[xxxix] then for us to belong *for real*, we need to learn how to show up authentically and truly reach a point where we are comfortable in our own skin, so to speak, and comfortable with our story regardless of the challenges we might have faced or continue to face.

Coffeehouse Five–Greenwood, Franklin, & Bargersville, Indiana

Brian and Michelle Peters started a place called Coffehouse Five in 2014 in their home community of Greenwood, Indiana but much had led to that beginning for them. As they share on the Coffeehouse Five website *Our Story,* it was 1996 and their family and marriage were in crisis, due to struggles with addiction and broken trust between them. During that time, they found a way through together by leaning on their families, and a renewed faith that led to the next chapter for their family and their professions. Earlier in their marriage, Brian had been an attorney for ten years and operated a software company another five years. Coming through their struggles and renewing their commitments is a part of the Coffeehouse Five story as well.

The new chapter for the Peters began with Brian later attending seminary and eventually taking a pastoral staff role for 10 years at Community Church of Greenwood (CCG). Initially, CCG rented space in their facility to the Peters for the first Coffeehouse Five location. Following their start there, with the blessing of CCG, Brian and Michelle launched Coffeehouse Five at their first stand-alone location. The Peters then launched a church plant that initially met at CCG and then later within their Coffeehouse Five location. So rather than having a coffee shop in the church at CCG, they launched Coffeehouse Five, then a church and began providing a location in town that was both their business as well as a place to offer ministry and services to their community.

In recent years, they have opened two additional coffee locations in Central Indiana that are a part of fueling the mission of Coffeehouse Five which is a "For Benefit" coffeehouse. As a *For Benefit* organization, "their net revenue funds...five initiatives for building a stronger community."[xl] The initiatives relate to relationship development (premarital counseling, marriage counseling), addiction recovery programs, mentor training, and giving each month to funding other mental health needs in their community. Their business has grown and so has their commitment to serving their community. Being an authentic couple, who have used their story and lessons learned to serve others gives a greater sense of belonging and purpose to customers and friends who are blessed to enter their doors. They offer more than the coffee, and house-made baked goods. They offer hope, support, and yes, love to their community. Community, connection and belonging are present at Coffeehouse Five and are also key ingredients to finding joy in places and in our lives.

Many seem to believe that the road to contentment is having or getting more. In my travels on *The Coffee Tour* this past two years, and simultaneously traveling my own journey of grief and loss, the list that leads to contentment does not seem to *require* these things. In fact, the list of what is priceless to me grows shorter all the time.

Do I like new, shiny, and beautiful things and places? Of course, I do! But contentment for me has not been as much about the externals as it has increasingly been about people, family, friends, and having a sense of place and belonging. We often hear people say that they want to "be a part of something that is bigger than themselves." While it can sound cliché to say it, I have found it to be true whether it is someone running a coffee shop in their hometown, volunteering in their community to paint, plant flowers, serving on a non-profit board, or mentoring a student. There is an intangible joy that can come from focusing our attention and service on "we" things rather than "me" things. As I have said before, I really do believe we are made for community, rather than isolation and being alone. That isn't to say that everyone needs to be an extrovert like me and talk a lot to people I know (and don't know!). Across the spectrum of personality and social space, belonging can look different in one place than it does in another. Sometimes, having a sense of belonging can be as simple as being known and appreciated in the places we go.

Warnick states that we sometimes establish "commercial friendships" that she says are "symptomatic of a pervasive modern loneliness. Lacking real friends, we seek social connection with shopkeepers and baristas."[xli] While this may be true, her perspective is that commercial friendships help us build a network of weak ties, "the casual relationships... social relationships that make us feel woven into the mesh of our city's daily life."[xlii] While I value strong ties, and deep roots in the community where I live, I do believe that social connection and the weak ties she talks about, can move us closer to those around us. When we share community space, we can tend to learn more of the stories of those who might initially be a commercial friendship, and then progress to a friendship that is rooted and strong, the kind that has staying power and links us more closely to the places we live and do business. "Place attachment research shows that many of the good feelings we have about the cities where we live stem from the sense that we have relationships there."[xliii]

Refinery Coffee Company–Goshen, IN

During my travels visiting coffee shops, I made a stop in Goshen, Indiana to visit a café called Electric Brew and meet a friend to explore the café in this cozy little town in Northeast Indiana. As we were discussing the Coffee Tour and the places I had been, my friend mentioned that if my schedule allowed that I should make a stop at Refinery Coffee Company on the edge of town. Having some extra time that day, I looked up the address, and headed to the location near the railroad tracks. I pulled into the lot outside of Refinery Coffee, located in an industrial-looking building. I initially wasn't sure if I had the right location but sure enough I did. Entering the front door, I walked into their lobby with all the various coffees, and retail items displayed. I was greeted by Marlene who is a sister of the owner. I briefly shared with her that I was doing a multi-state coffee tour and working on a book about the journey. She asked me if I would like to meet the owner, who happened to be there. I was introduced to Regina Troyer, who owns and founded the company in 2005. Initially, Refinery Coffee was a café location with food and coffee but over time Regina determined that the direction for her and the company was to transition to primarily being a roastery and distributor of coffee to their region. This transition took place in 2010, and the business moved to their current location, which has room to grow both in the roasting and distribution space, along with creating a retail shop where they will continue to offer coffee, merchandise, and espresso machines that they sell to cafes, and restaurants across the U.S.

When I visited and interviewed owners at coffee shops and roasteries, I typically asked them about how they have connected with their customers, built a following, built their brand, and built a community. In a follow up interview with Regina weeks later, she described how much she enjoys the education component of what she is doing. For example, as a community business, most of their clientele has grown out of personal referrals, word-of-mouth recommendations, promotions at local events, and limited direct marketing.

Examples of educational opportunities for Regina are multiple. As a distributor of espresso machines also, she typically goes to other cafés who buy their equipment from Refinery, and trains other baristas on using the machines in their own cafes.

One of the things she mentioned when I asked her about community and connection, was that her approach is to not only provide quality roasted coffees from their location, but with the education component it enables her customers to take home Refinery Coffee and prepare it in their homes with family and friends. By doing so, she is creating community and connections in other places as an extension of her business and passion for coffee.

The Refinery has grown since my first visit, and their location now includes an expanded retail space, with in-house educational opportunities for customers, prospective clients, and aspiring baristas. Along with all her success at Refinery Coffee Roasters, there is a connected story about Regina's upbringing and growing up in community.

According to Eric Wesner, there are over 28,000 Amish living in two northern Indiana counties of Elkhart & LaGrange that were founded in 1841[xliv]. Among them are Regina's family of origin. She was raised in the Indiana Amish community, one of six children in their family. Though she opted to live outside the Amish community when she became an adult, her love and appreciation for her heritage, faith and family is evident. She stated that growing up Amish "taught her a sense of community and belonging" and that she wished her children could have experienced her upbringing.[xlv]

Years later, she is a successful entrepreneur who loves people, her community and how coffee brings people together. Clearly, Regina has brought a sense of community and belonging to Refinery Coffee Company, and its reach continues to expand as the scope of her business and personal impact continue to grow.

Part III

Coming Home

As you know, the subtitle to this work is: *Rediscovering Community, Connection, and Belonging.* Throughout my writing there have been stages of insights, dry periods where the words did not come easily, and others where my thoughts would flow out of a conversation with a trusted friend or mentor. In the process of that, I have increasingly felt like these three factors (community, connection and belonging) have an interplay or an intersection where the three values are greater than any one of them separately. The overlapping circles represent each one looking something like this graphic at the right.

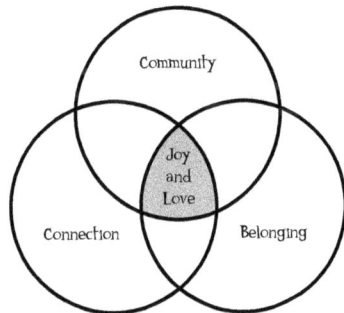

Community

Joy
and
Love

Connection   Belonging

With one circle representing community, another connection, and the third one belonging, there leaves an essential space in the center that joins all three.

Joy and love

Perhaps at the center of these three is where we experience joy and even love? Can there be joy without love, or love without joy? It could be love given and received in the form of a person, or a beloved animal or pet. Or it could be love in the form of an experience (music, art, solitude or reflection in a special place). I don't believe that we can experience joy without love in some form or another. Love given and love received is a beautiful reciprocity that fills our hearts. Even if joy is brief or short-lived, it seems like there must be at least a moment of love, being loved, and feeling loved every now and then. My experience has been, that because of this, we can experience joy and grief on the same day, perhaps moments apart. However, during our times of grief we can more likely survive that grief if we have moments of love and joy mixed in.

From the previously cited Harvard study as well as numerous other related studies over the last 90 years, "bear witness to the importance of human connections. They show that people who are more connected to family, to friends, and to community, are happier and physically healthier than people who are less connected."[xlvi]

At the intersection of community, connection, and belonging is not just joy *but the need for love, and to be loved.* When we embrace community, connection, and belonging, and help others experience what that feels like there can be joy (for us and for them).

Love and joy help the hard times be more bearable, even grief (with a progressive process of healing), can eventually present itself in different ways, rather than the raw, searing ache of loss being a permanent, disabling condition that we live with every day.

Growing Around Grief

Tonkin's model[xlvii] speaks to how we can grow over time, in spite of the grief we may be carrying. While we often hear that "time heals" her approach differs yet provides encouragement that growing with our grief can be a part of the journey. A visual representation looks like this:

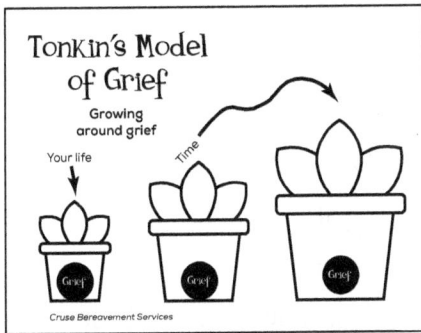

As it says in the model, we can grow around grief rather than thinking it just goes away (it doesn't). In retrospect, I think *The Coffee Tour* was a part of processing an extended period of grief from losing my parents, and at that time, it was very hard to feel love or give love. In my woundedness and grief, the tendency was to pull away as if my pain could be escaped somehow. However, as I traveled alone from state to state, café to café, I was reminded that through hospitality and warmth (mostly from people who didn't know me), I was offered kindness, and a welcome that was desperately needed.

Author, Laura Warfel, who is a friend, and former co-worker of mine, stated it in this way. "In the rush of daily life, we often don't take time to offer kindness and welcome. We either assume the other person feels this...or we ignore the needs of each person for these basic qualities of life."[xlviii]

In addition, along the way I connected with long-time friends and former students who I had not seen in a long time. Embracing those friendships and adding sweet memories in cafés across America, was a part of the search for community, and connection that I sometimes thought had been lost forever. I was finding short-term doses of it as I traveled but still there was an emptiness that remained. I could feel connection and experience community when I was in a place with other people, but at the same time they were not places of permanence, places I planned to stay, or really belonged, because it wasn't really my home.

"People benefit from deep and meaningful conversations that help us forge connections with one another, but we often stick to small talk with strangers because we underestimate how much others are interested in our lives and wrongly believe that deeper conversations will be more awkward and less enjoyable than they actually are."[xlix] Moving from town to town, there were some lovely, deep conversations but some also fit the description above, just small talk.

Where is Home?

I later realized that what I was looking for was much more than simply being in interesting places with other people but instead I was searching to find a real and lasting sense of belonging again, searching for home. Over the many miles and states I traveled, I had to reconcile quite a lot within my own heart and mind and prepare for the next chapter of my life. It turns out that was the hardest part. Rediscovering joy and love was an unseen work that needed to happen in my soul and spirit. Doing so would require much more of me than even my fifteen state Coffee Tour.

So, if I could feel community and connection at times during my travels, but not a lasting sense of belonging, where was that going to come from, and how was that supposed to take place? To answer that question, I had to heal more and seek that *internal* place within me that recognized *that I belonged* no matter where I was or who I was with (or not with) at that moment. I was seeking answers outside of me, in interesting places I enjoyed, but increasingly I began to realize those answers needed to be rediscovered *within me* not just *around* me.

For years, I have half-jokingly referred to myself as a "recovering perfectionist" but I truly do view it that way. For too many years, both personally and professionally, I sought to always make the right call, always have it together, always say and do the perfect thing. I think it often led me to being a cheap imitation of myself. I thought if I looked the part, and showed absolute confidence, that it would help me be successful. But the truth is, that was so wrong!

Even with terrific role models (some right in my own family), as well as leaders and friends in my life throughout my personal and professional journey, the only *perfecting process* I could hope for was to become the very best, most kind, helpful and authentic ME possible. I had to let go of the myth of perfection.

Stephen Graves, in his book "Flourishing" (2014) states: "It takes a lifetime to become authentic...but the sooner we forget about mimicking other voices and begin cultivating our own, the sooner we find fulfillment."[1] A part of reaching that point of authenticity and self-acceptance, is to not just accept but *embrace* the fact that I am flawed and imperfect, but that doesn't mean I have to live my life in the vast sea of feeling like I don't measure up. I do not have to live in the misperception that I'm not good enough in whatever my current pursuits are. Do I still struggle at times and need to get better and grow in my journey? 100%! Just ask those who know me best but choose to love me anyway (thank you for this gift).

Foundations

When it comes to the matter of my internal sense of belonging and feeling like *I can be enough in this world*, that leads me to my foundation of faith and belief. That may not be your story and matters of faith are not something of great interest to you. But for me to summarize my Joy Café journey to this point, I would invite you to stay with me for the remaining pages.

As the months of 2021 and 2022 were grinding along, with grief ever-present, there was a long season of thinking about matters of faith in God, my place in this world, what it all meant in the scope of my life, and if it was truly a foundation that I could stake my life and soul upon.

My growing up family was a strong Christian home, with loving, faithful parents who caused me to often say, "I hit the jackpot" when it came to parents and siblings. I am so grateful for that foundation and the teaching of countless Biblical truths growing up, that have sustained me to this day. At the same time, when we are hurting deeply and it seems like our future may not hold much joy or promise, we can question those bedrock beliefs and principles gleaned from our past lives. I was no different during that time. I asked myself hard questions about what I wanted the rest of my life to look like and prayed for relief from my grief and present circumstances. I was seeking a way to again experience joy in my life. I wanted to go home.

The good news is, that I have found my way back to joy in my life for many reasons, and it isn't one magic formula, but the keys I've talked about in this project of community, connection, and belonging are certainly a major part of what has brought me through to the other side, so to speak. If you are reading this, it will come as no surprise by now, that I believe all three are essential in our lives and keys to wellness, thriving, and joy! I hope that I have given you enough examples, resources and insights for you to find the joy you seek in your own life and in the lives you impact. The bottom line for me is this: we all need community, connection, and a sense of belonging. Also, finding joy in life is both an *internal work* and an *external work* that is likely a lifelong process. My sincere belief is that it takes both internal work (within me) and external work (around me) that will not happen by chance or by nature. It will typically require intentional, reflective work, soul searching, and realizing that most of life and my purpose for being here on this planet, is really not about ME.

Reflecting on my values, their place, and application to my everyday life, is internal work. Considering my closely held values and beliefs allows me to seek and find clarity; to keep what has lasting value and discarding those things that do not. What principles do I stand on without wavering, and what is the kind of person I want to be, despite my imperfections and flaws? Do I really live out my values daily or simply talk about them? And what do I do when I fall short of my desired and intended outcomes or responses? Do I respond in humility or become defensive? For years I have been working on getting better at saying, "I'm sorry, I was wrong, please forgive me." Though they are difficult words to say, those seven words go a long way in establishing or restoring relationships and partnerships. It's still a work in progress for me; but it is worth it.

As I have done the internal work around considering and affirming my values, I continually ask myself if I am being trustworthy, ethical, fair, loyal, honest, and sincere (among others)? Am I living out these concepts and showing up as the person I want to be, and who others believe me to be? It is not always popular to espouse boundaries, limits, standards, or morals when the general culture sometimes seems morally adrift or at least avoiding any limits on their chosen way of living. I choose to believe that we must have a foundation of values, faith, and morals that can sustain us through the many seasons of life. Otherwise, we are likely to join those who are adrift without a clear foundation, direction, or sense of purpose.

Another form of internal work was examining my faith (past and present), looking for answers and sources of truth, and reflecting on what I bring to this world that is unique to me. Without a frequent and sincere renewal and refocus on my faith, I would likely just walk away and give up on things ever making sense.

Actions rooted in faith that sustain me are: focused times of prayer, listening in silence and not being afraid of what I might hear or sense in that moment, practicing discernment and seeking wise counsel. Stanley suggests in "The Best Question Ever" that we ask "Is it wise?"[li] Many things may be legal, permissible, or acceptable to society *but is it wise?* That question has been a reliable, personal guardrail many times.

Finally, I wholeheartedly advocate journaling frequently or meeting regularly with a small group of close friends to get your thoughts, ideas, questions, doubts and feelings out of your head. Those trusted friends are what I call my Personal Board of Directors. Those trusted friends can serve as a sounding board for ideas, or a voice of reason when we are looking at potentially unwise actions or not thinking clearly.

For me writing things down in the quiet of the day, I can get those things out of my head or sketched onto a page that is a safe space. If you are a verbal processor, it may be that conversation with a close friend or group of friends, that help you evaluate next steps in your journey.

In my executive coaching practice, I often hear clients talk about getting "stuck in my own head" and not having a healthy, active practice to process those thoughts. I believe we are not meant to carry these weights alone, or in isolation and it continues to be an honor to "ride along" with those clients and friends.

We hear a lot of talk in books, articles, and the media about being authentic, and "keeping it real." One of the challenges is to define what that looks like and how it may be different for each of us. Is authenticity being open, vulnerable and sharing *everything* we think and feel with *everyone?* I don't think so. Emotional intelligence and filters certainly help in selecting when, what, and to whom we share our real selves.

I was facilitating a leadership training session recently, and one of our guest speakers stated that "peopling is hard" and it can be! Much like the internal work detailed above, we have the opportunity to do sincere work to grow, heal, and improve the connections we have with those in our families, our closest friends, and colleagues. I frequently state that "relationships are everything" because there is so much we can do in the context of healthy relationships to elevate others, inspire, collaborate, and solve problems together. Look no further than politics, government, or organizations that seem to believe the opposite and practice the habits of destruction, defeating, and demonizing those who don't agree with them. Positive and long-lasting results rarely come from that type of strategy.

Having entered my sixth decade of life, I often find myself considering the place and role of my work, how my remaining career and work life resonates with my mission of investing in others, helping them grow, learning, thriving, and maximizing their unique gifts, talents and strengths.

What's Next?

If you think about our lives and work as a series of chapters or seasons, with each one containing gains and losses, then there are some realities that we need to face. Arthur Brooks (2022) describes a concept introduced by Cattell that posits that we have two types of intelligence during our work life.[lii] The impact of each varies at different stages of our lives. The first curve he calls the stage of our *fluid intelligence*, and the second curve he calls *crystallized intelligence*. Fluid intelligence relates to our ability to "reason, think flexibly, and solve novel problems" (Cattell, 1971). The perspective given is that we thrive more on our fluid intelligence earlier in our working lives, and it is used the most in our striving years of earlier career and desired accomplishments. Crystallized intelligence, on the other hand, is making use of the body of knowledge we have learned in the past and the key is making a transition from one to the other. Considering this, as we head into our forties, fifties and sixties while our fluid intelligence tends to decline, our crystallized intelligence does not until much later in life. He describes this as leaping from one curve to the other, and knowing when it is time to do so.

Carrying forward the concept of crystallized intelligence, I have more working years behind me than I have in front of me. That can sound sad or perhaps forlorn, but the upside of that reality is that I have more to offer others than I would have even ten or fifteen years ago. I realized long ago that the bottom line is that all of this (work, impact, relationships, service) is that *it's really not about me!* For too long, I didn't realize that but now I certainly do. For several years, I had a phrase on my office wall that read "The audience is the HERO". In other words, those who listen to any message I might have, are the ones who can have the greatest impact in the world because it is multiplied *in them* not me.

Another way I can capitalize on my crystallized intelligence is by increasingly focusing on serving in my community. This can look like many different things, but for me it is giving of my time and resources to local ministries and non-profits. By doing so, I have learned so much about the needs, the people, the pain, the history, and the aspirations of those around me in my community. This has led me to do more than just making a donation each year (though I encourage that also) but also giving of a precious resource which is my time. When we show up for others and seek to make their lives better through our presence, and service (even in small ways), we turn our attention from ourselves. Doing so frequently increases our own sense of gratitude for who and what we have in our lives, and hopefully betters the lives of others.

If you have made it this far, you may be looking for the recipe or an exact pathway to joy. Honestly, there is no "silver bullet", but I do wholeheartedly believe that the answers are within your grasp. For my journey, the pillars of values, faith, relationships, vocational mission, community engagement, and serving others were the keys for my journey back to joy. My heart's desire is that if you are still seeking joy in your life, or needing to rediscover it, that you will do the work inside you, engage those who love and care about you, and find your path to joy. That you will find your way home.

References

Behar, H. (2007). *It's Not About the Coffee: Leadership Principles from a Life at Starbucks.* Penguin House: New York.

Birnstengal, G. (2020), January 17). What has the U.K.s minister of loneliness done to date? Next Avenue, https://www.nextavenue.org/uk-minister-of-loneliness.

Britannica, T. *Editors of Encyclopaedia* (2023, August 3). Nashville. Encyclopedia Britannica. https://www.britannica.com/place/Nashville-Indiana

Brooks, (2022). *From Strength to Strength: Finding Success, Happiness, and Deep Purpose in the Second Half of Life.* Penguin Random House: New York

Brown, B. (2021). *Atlas of the Heart: Mapping Meaningful Connection and the Language of Human Experience,* Random House: New York.

Cattell, R. B. (1961). Fluid and Crystallized Intelligence. In Brooks, (2022). *From Strength to Strength: Finding Success, Happiness, and Deep Purpose in the Second Half of Life.* Penguin Random House: New York

Clifton, J. (2022). *Blind Spot: The Global Rise of Unhappiness and How Leaders Missed it.* Gallup Press.

Derr, V. Children's Sense of Place in Northern New Mexico, March 2002. *Journal of Environmental Psychology,* 22 (1-2): 125-137.

Epley N, & Schroeder J. Mistakenly seeking solitude. *Journal of Experimental Psychology.* (2014 Oct;14) 3(5):1980-99.

Florida, R. (2009). *Who's Your City?: How the Creative Economy is Making Where to Live the Most Important Decision in Your Life.* New York: Basic.

Graves, S.R. (2015). Flourishing: Why Some People Thrive While Others Just Survive.

Good News Network, https://www.goodnewsnetwork.org/benefits-of-deep-conversations-with-strangers/

Holt-Lunstad, J., Smith, T. B., Baker, M., Harris, T., & Stephenson, D. (2015). Loneliness and social isolation as risk factors for mortality: A meta-analytic review. *Perspectives on Psychological Science,* 10, 227-237.

Kardas, M. Kumar, A. Epley, N. Overly Shallow? Miscalibrated Expectations Create a Barrier to Deeper Conversation. *Journal of Personality and Social Psychology,* Sept. 2021.

Marci, C.D. (2022). *Rewired: Protecting Your Brain in the Digital Age.* Harvard University Press, Cambridge, MA.

Murthy, V., Work and the loneliness epidemic. *Harvard Business Review,* September 26, 2017.

Newton, R. Rediscover Joy at Work, *Harvard Business Review,* September 08, 2021.

Parrott, L. & Parrott, L. (2011). *Real Relationships: From Better to Best, and Good to Great.* Zondervan Publishing.

Perrell, K. (2021). *Jump: Dare to Do What Scares You in Business & Life.* HarperCollins Leadership, New York.

Stanley, A. (2004). *The Best Question Ever; A Revolutionary Approach to Decision Making.* Random House, New York.

Tonkin, L. (1996) Growing around grief—another way of looking at grief and recovery, *Bereavement Care,* 15:1, 10.

Waldinger, R. & Schulz, M. (2023). *The Good Life: Lessons from the World's Longest Scientific Study of Happiness.* Simon & Schuster, New York.

Warnick, M. (2016). *This is Where you Belong: Finding Home Wherever You Live.* Penguin Books, New York, NY.

Welch, R. (1982). *We Really Do Need Each Other.* Zondervan: Grand Rapids, MI

Wesner, E. (2023). *Indiana Amish.* https://amishamerica.com/indiana-amish/

Williams, D. (2017). *What I Found in a Thousand Towns: A Traveling Musician's Guide to Rebuilding America's Communities.* Basic Books: New York, NY.

Endnotes

[i] Britannica, T. *Editors of Encyclopaedia* (2023, August 3). Nashville. Encyclopedia Britannica. https://www.britannica.com/place/Nashville-Indiana

[ii] Brown, B. (2021). *Atlas of the Heart: Mapping Meaningful Connecton and the Language of Human Experience*, Random House: New York.

[iii] Williams, D. (2017). *What I Found in a Thousand Towns: A Traveling Musician's Guide to Rebuilding America's Communites.* Basic Books: New York, NY.

[iv] Brown, B. (2021). *Atlas of the Heart: Mapping Meaningful Connecton and the Language of Human Experience*, Random House: New York.

[v] Newton, R. Rediscover Joy at Work, *Harvard Business Review*, September 08, 2021.

[vi] Epley N, & Schroeder J. Mistakenly seeking solitude. *Journal of Experimental Psychology.* (2014 Oct;14) 3(5):1980-99.

[vii] Brown, B. (2021). *Atlas of the Heart: Mapping Meaningful Connecton and the Language of Human Experience*, Random House: New York. p. 206.

[viii] Warnick, M. (2016). *This is Where you Belong: Finding Home Wherever You Live*Penguin Books, New York, NY.

[ix] Williams, D. (2017). *What I Found in a Thousand Towns: A Traveling Musician's Guide to Rebuilding America's Communites.* Basic Books: New York, NY. p.141.

[x] Williams, D. (2017). *What I Found in a Thousand Towns: A Traveling Musician's Guide to Rebuilding America's Communites.* Basic Books: New York, NY. p.xii.

[xi] Williams, D. (2017). *What I Found in a Thousand Towns: A Traveling Musician's Guide to Rebuilding America's Communites.* Basic Books: New York, NY. p.xii.

[xii] Williams, D. (2017). *What I Found in a Thousand Towns: A Traveling Musician's Guide to Rebuilding America's Communites.* Basic Books: New York, NY. p.11-12.

[xiii] Brown, B. (2021). *Atlas of the Heart: Mapping Meaningful Connecton and the Language of Human Experience*, Random House: New York. p. 170.

[xiv] Murthy, V., Work and the loneliness epidemic. *Harvard Business Review,* September 26, 2017.

[xv] Epley N, & Schroeder J. Mistakenly seeking solitude. *Journal of Experimental Psychology.* (2014 Oct;14) 3(5):1980-99.

[xvi] Brown, B. (2021). *Atlas of the Heart: Mapping Meaningful Connecton and the Language of Human Experience*, Random House: New York. p.169

xvii   Clifon, J. (2022). Blind Spot: *The Global Rise of Unhappiness and How Leaders Missed it.* Gallup Press.

xviii   Birnstengal, G. (2020), January 17). What has the U.K.s minister of loneliness done to date? Next Avenue, htps://www.nextavenue.org/uk-minister-of-loneliness.

xix   Birnstengal, G. (2020), January 17). What has the U.K.s minister of loneliness done to date? Next Avenue, htps://www.nextavenue.org/uk-minister-of-loneliness.

xx   Marci, C.D. (2022). *Rewired: Protectng Your Brain in the Digital Age.* Harvard University Press, Cambridge, MA. p. 157.

xxi   Brown, B. (2021). *Atlas of the Heart: Mapping Meaningful Connecton and the Language of Human Experience,* Random House: New York. p.255

xxii   Frunze, Stefan & Ari, (2021). Personal Communicaton

xxiii   Brown, B. (2021). *Atlas of the Heart: Mapping Meaningful Connecton and the Language of Human Experience,* Random House: New York. p. 155

xxiv   Murthy, V., Work and the loneliness epidemic. *Harvard Business Review,* September 26, 2017.

xxv   Brown, B. (2021). *Atlas of the Heart: Mapping Meaningful Connecton and the Language of Human Experience,* Random House: New York. p. 154.

xxvi   Derr, V. Children's Sense of Place in Northern New Mexico, March 2002. *Journal of Environmental Psychology,* 22 (1-2): p. 131.

xxvii   Florida, R. (2009). Who's Your City?: *How the Creatve Economy is Making Where to Live the Most Important Decision in Your Life.* New York: Basic.

xxviii   Warnick, M. (2016). *This is Where you Belong: Finding Home Wherever You Live.* Penguin Books, New York, NY. p. 15.

xxix   Williams, D. (2017). *What I Found in a Thousand Towns: A Traveling Musician's Guide to Rebuilding America's Communites.* Basic Books: New York, NY. p.78.

xxx   Williams, D. (2017). *What I Found in a Thousand Towns: A Traveling Musician's Guide to Rebuilding America's Communites.* Basic Books: New York, NY. p.91.

xxxi   Williams, D. (2017). *What I Found in a Thousand Towns: A Traveling Musician's Guide to Rebuilding America's Communites.* Basic Books: New York, NY. p.94.

xxxii   Williams, D. (2017). *What I Found in a Thousand Towns: A Traveling Musician's Guide to Rebuilding America's Communites.* Basic Books: New York, NY. p.88.

xxxiii Williams, D. (2017). *What I Found in a Thousand Towns: A Traveling Musician's Guide to Rebuilding America's Communites.* Basic Books: New York, NY. p.131.

xxxiv Brown, B. (2021). *Atlas of the Heart: Mapping Meaningful Connecton and the Language of Human Experience,* Random House: New York. p. 154.

xxxv Waldinger, R. & Schulz, M. (2023). *The Good Life: Lessons from the World's Longest Scientfc Study of Happiness.* Simon & Schuster, New York. p. 3

xxxvi Waldinger, R. & Schulz, M. (2023). *The Good Life: Lessons from the World's Longest Scientfc Study of Happiness.* Simon & Schuster, New York. p. 21

xxxvii Welch, R. (1982). *We Really Do Need Each Other.* Zondervan: Grand Rapids, MI

xxxviii Brown, B. (2021). *Atlas of the Heart: Mapping Meaningful Connecton and the Language of Human Experience,* Random House: New York. p. 158-159

xxxix Brown, B. (2021). *Atlas of the Heart: Mapping Meaningful Connecton and the Language of Human Experience,* Random House: New York. p. 172.

xl Coffeehouse Five, Franklin, Indiana. www.cofeehousefve.com

xli Warnick, M. (2016). *This is Where you Belong: Finding Home Wherever You Live.* Penguin Books, New York, NY. p. 57.

xlii Warnick, M. (2016). *This is Where you Belong: Finding Home Wherever You Live.* Penguin Books, New York, NY. p. 57.

xliii Warnick, M. (2016). *This is Where you Belong: Finding Home Wherever You Live.* Penguin Books, New York, NY. p. 70.

xliv Wesner, E. (2023). *Indiana Amish.* https://amishamerica.com/indiana-amish/

xlv Regina Troyer (2023). Personal Communicaton

xlvi Waldinger, R. & Schulz, M. (2023). *The Good Life: Lessons from the World's Longest Scientfc Study of Happiness.* Simon & Schuster, New York. p. 21

xlvii Tonkin, L. (1996) Growing around grief—another way of looking at grief and recovery, *Bereavement Care,* 15:1, 10.

xlviii Warfel, L. (2024). Personal Communicaton.

xlix Murthy, V., Work and the loneliness epidemic. *Harvard Business Review,* September 26, 2017. p.20

l Graves, S.R. (2015). Flourishing: Why Some People Thrive While Others Just Survive. p. 50

li   Stanley, A. (2004). *The Best Queston Ever; A Revolutonary Approach to Decision Making.* Random House, New York.

lii   lllBrooks, (2022). *From Strength to Strength: Finding Success, Happiness, and Deep Purpose in the Second Half of Life.* Penguin Random House: New York

liii   1Catell, R. B. (1961). Fluid and Crystallized Intelligence. In Brooks, (2022). From *Strength to Strength: Finding Success, Happiness, and Deep Purpose in the Second Half of Life.* Penguin Random House: New York.

The Coffee Tour Locations

Café Name	City	State
Onyx Coffee	Bentonville	AR
Airship Coffee	Bentonville	AR
Heroes Coffee	Bentonville	AR
Onyx Coffee Lab	Bentonville	AR
Meteor Café	Bentonville	AR
Onyx Coffee Lab-HQ	Rogers	AR
States Café	Benicia	CA
Café Bernardo	Davis	CA
The Buena Vista	San Francisco	CA
Con Azucar Café	San Jose	CA
Basque Boulangerie Café	Sonoma	CA
Sunflower Caffe	Sonoma	CA
Journey Café	Vacaville	CA
Cuba Café	Vacaville	CA
Black and Brew	Lakeland	FL
Flower Café	Orlando	FL
World of Coffee	Orlando	FL
Independent Grounds	Kennesaw	GA
Coffee Emporium	Iowa City	IA
Cody Road Coffee	LeClaire	IA
Bean and Barley	Ashkum	IL
Fort Jesse Café	Champaign/Urbana	IL
Cultivate Community Table	Frankfort	IL
Stefari West Avenue	Kankakee	IL
Café Di Moda	Lisle	IL
Gost Coffee Roasters	New Lenox	IL
Cornerstone Coffee	Peotone	IL
Zion Coffee	Peoria	IL
Garden Table	Broad Ripple	IN

Crescendo Coffee	Fort Wayne	IN
Old Crown Coffee Roasters	Fort Wayne	IN
Friendly Fox	Fort Wayne	IN
Bon Bon Coffee	Fort Wayne	IN
Conjure Coffee	Fort Wayne	IN
Old Crown Coffee Roasters	Fort Wayne	IN
Friendly Fox	Fort Wayne	IN
Firefly Coffee	Fort Wayne	IN
Utopian Coffee	Fort Wayne	IN
Coffeehouse Five	Franklin	IN
Electric Coffee	Goshen	IN
Refinery Coffee	Goshen	IN
Coffeehouse Five	Greenwood	IN
Calvin Fletchers Coffee	Indianapolis	IN
Doubting Thomas Café	Kokomo	IN
Red Roaster Café	Madison	IN
Madison Coffee & Tea	Madison	IN
Rosebuds Coffee House	Muncie	IN
Rochester Bagel	Rochester	IN
Rivet Coffee	Westfield	IN
Uplift Coffee	Lawrence	KS
McClain Coffee	Lawrence	KS
Aldea Coffee	Grand Haven	MI
Infusco Coffee	Sawyer	MI
Lakota Coffee Company	Columbia	MO
Shortwave Coffee	Columbia	MO
Java Jive	Hannibal	MO
Mildreds	Kansas City	MO
Great Stone Coffee	Osage Beach	MO
Frontier Perk Café	St. Charles	MO
Bike Stop Café & Outpost	St. Charles	MO
Myrtle & Cypress	Omaha	NE
Warehouse 4	Kettering	OH

Beastro- Marshawn Lynch	Portland	OR
Portland Exchange	Portland	OR
Barista	Portland	OR
Plumb Line Coffee	Clarksville	TN

www.ingramcontent.com/pod-product-compliance
Lightning Source LLC
Chambersburg PA
CBHW060254030426
42335CB00014B/1689